Generation 1

1. **DANIEL¹ FLEMING** was born on 02 Apr 1796 in Nuneaton, Warwickshire, England. He died on 17 Apr 1845 in Milton, Halton, Ontario, Canada. He married Elizabeth Taylor, daughter of John Taylor Sr and Ann Sainsbury White, on 13 Jun 1820 in Bradford on Avon, Wiltshire, England. She was born on 28 May 1798 in Holt, Wiltshire, England. She died on 03 Nov 1878 in Milton, Halton, Ontario, Canada (Cause of Death: Typhoid Fever).

Daniel Fleming and Elizabeth Taylor had the following children:

2.   i.   SAMUEL² FLEMING was born on 05 Jul 1821 in Bradford on Avon, Wiltshire, England. He died on 18 Nov 1891 in Windsor, Essex, Ontario, Canada. He married Sophia Upton Harwood, daughter of Henry Harwood and Sophia Upton, on 06 Jun 1855 in Palermo, Halton, Canada West, Canada. She was born on 18 May 1828 in Palermo, Halton, Ontario, Canada. She died on 21 Dec 1915 in 183 Ouellette Av, Windsor, Essex, Ontario, Canada.

    ii.   ELLEN FLEMING was born on 09 May 1823 in Bradford on Avon, Wiltshire, England. She died on 10 Aug 1843 in Milton, Halton, Ontario, Canada. She married Joseph Martin, son of Jasper Martin and Sarah Coates, between 1842-1843 in Milton, Halton, Upper Canada, Canada. He was born on 29 Jan 1818 in Northumberland, England. He died on 03 Dec 1900 in Milton, Halton, Ontario, Canada.

    iii.   JENNETTE FLEMING was born on 09 Apr 1826 in Bradford on Avon, Wiltshire, England. She died on 09 Jun 1880 in Toronto, Ontario, Canada.

    iv.   EDWARD WHITE FLEMING was born on 22 Apr 1831 in Meadville, Crawford, Pennsylvania, USA. He died on 12 Jul 1900 in Milton, Halton, Ontario, Canada (Cause of Death: Msannia).

3.   v.   MARY ANN FLEMING was born on 14 Sep 1832 in Erie, Pennsylvania, USA. She died on 09 May 1906 in Adrian, Lenawee, Michigan, USA. She married Edward Martin, son of Jasper Martin and Sarah Coates, in 1851 in Milton, Halton, Canada West, Canada. He was born on 19 Nov 1822 in Milton, Halton, Upper Canada, Canada. He died on 22 Sep 1885 in Adrian, Lenawee, Michigan, USA.

4.   vi.   LUCY A FLEMING was born on 18 Jun 1835 in Pittsburgh, Allegheny, Pennsylvania, USA. She died on 05 Jan 1926 in Lawrence, Douglas, Kansas, USA. She married Julius Augustus Keeler, son of Lewis Beebe Keeler and Rebecca Stevens, on 08 May 1873 in Olathe, Johnson, Kansas, USA. He was born on 28 Apr 1832 in Norwalk, Huron, Ohio, USA. He died on 07 Apr 1920 in Garden City, Finney, Kansas, USA.

    vii.   ELIZABETH FLEMING was born on 27 Mar 1841 in Milton, Halton, Upper Canada, Canada. She died on 27 Jul 1923 in Leamington, Essex, Ontario, Canada. She married Upton Harwood, son of Henry Harwood and Sophia Upton, on 12 Sep 1872 in Halton, Ontario, Canada. He was born on 28 Jan 1839 in Palermo, Halton, Ontario, Canada. He died on 03 Mar 1899 in Leamington, Essex, Ontario, Canada.

Generation 2

2. **SAMUEL² FLEMING** (Daniel¹) was born on 05 Jul 1821 in Bradford on Avon, Wiltshire, England. He died on 18 Nov 1891 in Windsor, Essex, Ontario, Canada. He married Sophia Upton Harwood, daughter of Henry Harwood and Sophia Upton, on 06 Jun 1855 in Palermo, Halton, Canada West, Canada. She was born on 18 May 1828 in Palermo, Halton, Ontario, Canada. She died on 21 Dec 1915 in 183 Ouellette Av, Windsor, Essex, Ontario, Canada.

Samuel Fleming and Sophia Upton Harwood had the following children:

5.   i.   ARTHUR SAMUEL HENRY³ FLEMING was born on 03 Apr 1856 in Milton, Halton, Ontario, Canada. He died on 11 Aug 1940 in Pasadena, Los Angeles, California, USA. He married Clara Huntington Fowler, daughter of Eldridge Merrick Fowler and Mary Louise Skinner, on 30 Nov 1892 in Chicago, Cook, Illinois, USA. She was born on 12 Feb 1866 in Bay City, Bay, Michigan, USA. She died on 29 Nov 1904 in San Francisco, California, USA.

ii. DONALD HOLTON WILLIAM UPTON FLEMING was born on 24 Mar 1857 in Milton, Halton, Ontario, Canada. He died on 18 Mar 1880 in Windsor, Essex, Ontario, Canada (Occupation: Bank Clerk for Milton Hahn Co. ; Cause of Death: Tuberculosis Pulmonary for two years.).

iii. LILLA ELIZABETH FLEMING was born on 15 May 1858 in Milton, Halton, Ontario, Canada. She died on 18 Mar 1886 in Allegan, Michigan, USA. She married George Calder Palmer on 26 Oct 1880 in Windsor, Essex, Ontario, Canada. He was born about 1852 in Ontario, Canada.

6. iv. BERTHA ANN HARWOOD FLEMING was born on 27 Jun 1859 in Milton, Halton, Canada West, Canada. She died on 17 Dec 1934 in Pasadena, Los Angeles, California, USA. She married August Karl Stellwagen LLD, son of Michael Von Stellwagen and Anna Elisabetha Endlich, on 03 Mar 1887 in Detroit, Wayne, Michigan, USA. He was born on 17 Feb 1849 in Nieder Saulheim, Hessen, Germany. He died on 13 Jun 1926 in Detroit, Wayne, Michigan, USA.

7. v. OSCAR ERNEST FLEMING LLD was born on 17 Mar 1862 in Milton, Halton, Ontario, Canada. He died on 29 Nov 1944 in Toronto, Ontario, Canada. He married Alice Whitney, daughter of William Howell Drake MD and Maria Augusta Ambridge, on 12 Feb 1890 in Kingsville, Essex, Ontario, Canada. She was born on 08 Sep 1867 in Kingsville, Essex, Ontario, Canada. She died in 1955 in Windsor, Essex, Ontario, Canada (Saint Johns Anglican Church Cemetery, Windsor, Essex County, Ontario, Canada).

8. vi. HARWOOD ONTARIO OSBORNE FLEMING was born on 15 Nov 1862 in Milton, Halton, Ontario, Canada. He died on 02 Jun 1937 in Riverside, Riverside, California, USA. He married (1) JANET GRAHAM CAMPBELL, daughter of George Campbell and Fanny Hannah Campbell, on 11 Feb 1896 in 237 London St, Windsor, Essex, Ontario, Canada. She was born on 25 Apr 1871 in Windsor, Essex, Ontario, Canada. She died on 28 Dec 1953 in Riverside, Yolo, California, USA.

9. vii. CLARENCE URIEL SIMCOE BRONTE FLEMING was born on 21 Aug 1866 in Bronte, Canada West, Canada. He died on 17 Nov 1941 in Pasadena, Los Angeles, California, USA. He married Mabel Rogers Taylor, daughter of Frank Dwight Taylor and Phebe Elizabeth Shords, on 08 Nov 1900 in Detroit, Wayne, Michigan, USA. She was born on 15 Dec 1873 in Detroit, Wayne, Michigan, USA. She died on 20 Jul 1941 in 224 Oak Lawn Av, Pasadena, Los Angeles, California, USA.

10. viii. SARAH FELICIA LOUISA PELL FLEMING was born on 16 Sep 1867 in Bronte, Halton, Ontario, Canada. She died on 26 Jun 1928 in Toronto, Ontario, Canada. She married (2) RICHARD HURON HOLMES, son of Thomas Holmes LLD and Elizabeth Lane, on 15 Nov 1887 in Windsor, Essex, Ontario, Canada. He was born on 06 Mar 1856 in Toronto, Ontario, Canada. He died on 05 Oct 1933 in Toronto, Ontario, Canada.

11. ix. FLORENCE SELENICA VIOLA FLEMING was born on 10 Aug 1869 in Walkerville, Essex, Ontario, Canada. She died on 25 Mar 1965 in Riverside, Yolo, California, USA. She married William Everette Scotten, son of Walter Scotten and Martha E McCard, on 16 Sep 1891 in Essex, Ontario, Canada. He was born on 17 Jul 1857 in Quincy, Houghton, Michigan, USA. He died on 19 May 1945 in Pasadena, Los Angeles, California, USA.

x. MARY EVELYN ISABELLA HAMILTON FLEMING was born on 06 May 1872 in Walkerville, Essex, Ontario, Canada. She died on 07 Jul 1936 in Detroit, Wayne, Michigan, USA. She married Albert George Theodore Montreuil, son of Luke Montreuil and Marie Therese Roberge, on 16 Jun 1896 in St Alphonsus Church, Windsor, Essex, Ontario, Canada. He was born on 29 Apr 1870 in Walkerville, Essex, Ontario, Canada. He died on 02 Oct 1936 in Riverside Dr, Windsor, Essex, Ontario, Canada.

3. MARY ANN^2 FLEMING (Daniel^1) was born on 14 Sep 1832 in Erie, Pennsylvania, USA. She died on

09 May 1906 in Adrian, Lenawee, Michigan, USA. She married Edward Martin, son of Jasper Martin and Sarah Coates, in 1851 in Milton, Halton, Canada West, Canada. He was born on 19 Nov 1822 in Milton, Halton, Upper Canada, Canada. He died on 22 Sep 1885 in Adrian, Lenawee, Michigan, USA.

Edward Martin and Mary Ann Fleming had the following children:

i. JOSEPH[3] MARTIN was born on 14 Sep 1852 in Milton, Halton, Upper Canada, Canada. He died on 02 Mar 1923 in Vancouver, British Columbia, Canada. He married Elizabeth Jane Rielly, daughter of Edward Rielly and Sarah Ann Bell, on 02 Sep 1881 in Carleton, Ontario, Canada. She was born in 1843 in Bells Corners, Nepean, Ottawa, Upper Canada, Canada. She died on 13 Feb 1913 in Lambeth, London, England.

12. ii. JASPER F MARTIN was born on 22 Jun 1854 in Milton, Halton, Canada West, Canada. He died on 09 Mar 1892 in Ypsilanti, Washtenaw, Michigan, USA (M T Conklin home, Congress & Summit Sts,). He married Eva E Rogers, daughter of Oscar K Rogers and Margaret L Cook, on 09 Sep 1879 in Washtenaw, Michigan, USA. She was born in 1859 in Ypsilanti, Washtenaw, Michigan, USA.

13. iii. EDWARD DANIEL MARTIN was born on 30 Sep 1856 in Milton, Halton, Canada West, Canada. He died on 14 May 1938 in Toronto, Ontario, Canada. He married Agnes Jane Perry, daughter of James Perry and Agnes Nancy Kerr, on 06 Aug 1879 in Ottawa, Ontario, Canada. She was born in May 1860 in Ottawa, Ontario, Canada. She died on 10 Dec 1945 in Forest Hill, Toronto, Ontario, Canada (Cause of Death: Old age).

iv. WILLIAM MARTIN was born on 27 Jul 1858 in Milton, Halton, Canada West, Canada. He died on 17 Apr 1874 in Augusta, Washtenaw, Michigan, USA.

v. GEORGE MARTIN was born on 10 Apr 1860 in Milton, Halton, Canada West, Canada. He died on 05 May 1862 in Milton, Halton, Canada West, Canada.

vi. FRANCIS DICKINS MARTIN was born on 22 Aug 1862 in Milton, Halton, Canada West, Canada. He died on 14 Jun 1866 in Ypsilanti, Washtenaw, Michigan, USA.

vii. ELLEN MARTIN was born on 10 Jun 1864 in Milton, Halton, Canada West, Canada. She died on 20 Jun 1864 in Milton, Halton, Canada West, Canada.

14. viii. MARY A MARTIN was born on 23 Sep 1865 in Ypsilanti, Washtenaw, Michigan, USA. She died on 19 Dec 1946 in San Diego, California, USA. She married Jerome W Robbins on 31 Jul 1897 in Lucas, Ohio, USA.

ix. CHARLES F MARTIN was born on 28 Jul 1868 in Ypsilanti, Washtenaw, Michigan, USA. He died on 19 Feb 1949 in Pontiac, Oakland, Michigan, USA.

x. JAMES WALKER MARTIN was born on 14 Nov 1870 in Augusta, Washtenaw, Michigan, USA. He died on 19 Dec 1933 in 7534 Burlington Dr, Detroit, Wayne, Michigan, USA.

4. LUCY A[2] FLEMING (Daniel[1]) was born on 18 Jun 1835 in Pittsburgh, Allegheny, Pennsylvania, USA. She died on 05 Jan 1926 in Lawrence, Douglas, Kansas, USA. She married Julius Augustus Keeler, son of Lewis Beebe Keeler and Rebecca Stevens, on 08 May 1873 in Olathe, Johnson, Kansas, USA. He was born on 28 Apr 1832 in Norwalk, Huron, Ohio, USA. He died on 07 Apr 1920 in Garden City, Finney, Kansas, USA.

Julius Augustus Keeler and Lucy A Fleming had the following children:

i. BEE KEELER was born on 29 Dec 1859 in Mound City, Linn, Kansas, USA. He died on 13 Nov 1931 in Garden City, Finney, Kansas, USA.

ii. MINNIE KEELER was born on 20 Aug 1861 in Lawrence, Douglas, Kansas, USA. She died in 1864 in Olathe, Johnson, Kansas, USA.

iii. MOLLIE KEELER was born on 10 Sep 1863 in Olathe, Johnson, Kansas, USA. She died in 1864 in Olathe, Johnson, Kansas, USA.

15. iv. EMMA KEELER was born on 09 Aug 1865 in Olathe, Johnson, Kansas, USA. She died on 06 Apr 1953. She married George T Emslie on 27 Oct 1884 in Johnson,

Kansas, USA. He was born about 1853 in England. He died in 1900.

    v.   JENNIE ELIZABETH KEELER was born on 14 Feb 1867 in Olathe, Johnson, Kansas, USA. She died on 04 Oct 1944 in Olathe, Johnson, Kansas, USA.

16.   vi.   JULIA AUGUSTA KEELER was born on 12 Jan 1869 in Olathe, Johnson, Kansas, USA. She died on 04 Oct 1944. She married John Alex Logan Boyd, son of Marshall Wesley Boyd and Minerva Richards, in 1884. He was born on 14 Oct 1865 in Creal Springs, Williamson, Illinois, USA. He died on 15 Oct 1942 in Springfield, Greene, Missouri, USA.

17.   vii.   LEWIS KEELER was born on 20 Aug 1870 in Olathe, Johnson, Kansas, USA. He died on 22 Jun 1953 in Garden City, Finney, Kansas, USA. He married Sadie Inez Davis, daughter of Roderick Ransom Davis and Nancy Sarah Aumiller, in Jan 1895 in Gray County, Kansas, USA. She was born on 08 Sep 1872 in Greenwood, Franklin, Kansas, USA. She died on 17 Aug 1956 in 5011 Pleasant St, Polk, Iowa, USA (died at home of daughter).

18.   viii.   ANNA DAVENPORT KEELER was born on 03 Dec 1872 in Olathe, Johnson, Kansas, USA. She died on 08 Sep 1957 in Lawrence, Douglas, Kansas, USA. She married Harry Burton White, son of Thomas King White and Sarah Ann Elizabeth Little, on 31 Dec 1895 in Wakefield, Clay, Kansas, USA. He was born on 11 Feb 1872 in Wakefield, Clay, Kansas, USA. He died on 19 Aug 1909 in Wakefield, Clay, Kansas, USA (Madura Cemetery, Wakefield, Clay County, Kansas, USA).

    ix.   MARY KEELER was born on 17 Aug 1875 in Olathe, Johnson, Kansas, USA. She died on 19 Aug 1875 in Olathe, Johnson, Kansas, USA.

    x.   AUGUSTUS KEELER was born on 24 Aug 1876 in Olathe, Johnson, Kansas, USA. He died on 25 Aug 1876 in Olathe, Johnson, Kansas, USA.

Generation 3

5.   **ARTHUR SAMUEL HENRY³ FLEMING** (Samuel², Daniel¹) was born on 03 Apr 1856 in Milton, Halton, Ontario, Canada. He died on 11 Aug 1940 in Pasadena, Los Angeles, California, USA. He married Clara Huntington Fowler, daughter of Eldridge Merrick Fowler and Mary Louise Skinner, on 30 Nov 1892 in Chicago, Cook, Illinois, USA. She was born on 12 Feb 1866 in Bay City, Bay, Michigan, USA. She died on 29 Nov 1904 in San Francisco, California, USA.

Arthur Samuel Henry Fleming and Clara Huntington Fowler had the following child:

19.   i.   MARJORIE⁴ FLEMING was born on 14 Oct 1894 in Detroit, Wayne, Michigan, USA. She died on 11 Apr 1985 in Palm Beach, Florida, USA. She married (1) WILTON LLOYD-SMITH, son of Walter Lloyd-Smith and Jessie E Gonzales, on 25 Aug 1917 in Pasadena, Los Angeles, California, USA. He was born on 24 May 1894 in Elmira Heights, Elmira, Chemung, New York, USA. He died on 29 Feb 1940 in Manhattan, New York, New York, USA (committed suicide.). She married (2) KNIGHT WOOLLEY. He was born on 01 May 1895 in Brooklyn, Kings, New York, USA. He died on 18 Jan 1984 in Hobe Sound, Martin, Florida, USA.

6.   **BERTHA ANN HARWOOD³ FLEMING** (Samuel², Daniel¹) was born on 27 Jun 1859 in Milton, Halton, Canada West, Canada. She died on 17 Dec 1934 in Pasadena, Los Angeles, California, USA. She married August Karl Stellwagen LLD, son of Michael Von Stellwagen and Anna Elisabetha Endlich, on 03 Mar 1887 in Detroit, Wayne, Michigan, USA. He was born on 17 Feb 1849 in Nieder Saulheim, Hessen, Germany. He died on 13 Jun 1926 in Detroit, Wayne, Michigan, USA.

August Karl Stellwagen LLD and Bertha Ann Harwood Fleming had the following child:

    i.   KARL DONALD⁴ STELLWAGON LLD was born on 05 Mar 1889 in Detroit, Wayne, Michigan, USA. He died on 27 Jan 1944 in Detroit, Wayne, Michigan, USA. He married Gladys M Zinn, daughter of Gustav Zinn Jr and Emma Theresia Anna Schwarm, on 06 Jul 1914 in Cuyahoga, Ohio, USA. She was born on 19 Sep 1894 in Detroit, Wayne, Michigan, USA. She died in May 1966 in Ludington, Mason,

Michigan, USA.

7. **OSCAR ERNEST³ FLEMING LLD** (Samuel², Daniel¹) was born on 17 Mar 1862 in Milton, Halton, Ontario, Canada. He died on 29 Nov 1944 in Toronto, Ontario, Canada. He married Alice Whitney, daughter of William Howell Drake MD and Maria Augusta Ambridge, on 12 Feb 1890 in Kingsville, Essex, Ontario, Canada. She was born on 08 Sep 1867 in Kingsville, Essex, Ontario, Canada. She died in 1955 in Windsor, Essex, Ontario, Canada (Saint Johns Anglican Church Cemetery, Windsor, Essex County, Ontario, Canada).

Oscar Ernest Fleming LLD and Alice Whitney had the following children:

i. CONSTANCE AUGUSTA⁴ FLEMING was born on 12 Dec 1890 in Windsor, Essex, Ontario, Canada. She died on 30 Jan 1969 in Mount Albert, York, Ontario, Canada.

20. ii. DONALD WILLIAM FLEMING was born on 25 Mar 1892 in Windsor, Essex, Ontario, Canada. He died on 20 Oct 1961 in Riverside Manor, Windsor, Essex, Ontario, Canada. He married Isabella Mary Blanchard, daughter of Louis Blanchard and Mary Ellen Tobin, on 04 Jun 1921 in Winnipeg, Manitoba, Canada. She was born on 05 Mar 1888 in Charlottenburgh, Glengarry, Ontario, Canada (Father: Louis Blanchard (1828-1903) / Mother: Mary Ellen Tobin (1842-1929)). She died on 07 Jul 1951 in Cantley, Les Collines-de-l'Outaouais, Quebec, Canada.

21. iii. FRANCES MAUD FLEMING was born on 08 Jan 1894 in Windsor, Essex, Ontario, Canada. She died on 21 Aug 1980 in Ottawa, Ontario, Canada. She married Harold George Kerrigan, son of James Kerrigan and Augusta Bryson Moore, on 18 Dec 1915 in Sandwich St W, Windsor, Essex, Ontario, Canada. He was born on 02 Jun 1879 in Toronto, Ontario, Canada. He died on 17 Feb 1928 in Los Angeles, California, USA.

iv. THELMA CAROLINE FLEMING was born on 13 Aug 1895 in Windsor, Essex, Ontario, Canada. She died on 12 Jun 1990 in St. Johns Churchyard, Windsor, Essex, Ontario, Canada.

22. v. OSCAR EDWARD SCOTTEN FLEMING LLD was born on 13 Feb 1897 in Windsor, Essex, Ontario, Canada. He died on 03 Jan 1957 in London, Middlesex, Ontario, Canada. He married (1) IRENE FAIRCLOUGH on 28 Jul 1927 in Windsor, Essex, Ontario, Canada. She was born about 1906 in Barnsley, Shropshire, England. She died in 1990. He married (2) JULIA ANTOINETTE CHANEL, daughter of Albert Chanel and Jeanne Eugenie DeVolle, on 11 Nov 1919 in Paris, Île-de-France, France. She was born on 13 Jun 1887 in Issoire, Puy-de-Dôme, Auvergne, France. She died on 02 May 1921 in Buenos Aires, Argentina.

23. vi. CANMORE DRAKE FLEMING was born on 02 Jan 1899 in Windsor, Essex, Ontario, Canada. He died on 08 Feb 1967 in Etobicoke, Toronto, Ontario, Canada. He married Evelyn Eileen Johnston, daughter of Arthur James Johnston and Amy Eliza Mason, on 23 May 1944 in Toronto, Ontario, Canada. She was born on 29 Dec 1903 in Toronto, Ontario, Canada. She died on 21 Feb 1976 in Toronto, Ontario, Canada.

24. vii. KENNETH ELDON FLEMING was born on 07 Nov 1900 in Windsor, Essex, Ontario, Canada. He died on 05 Oct 1965 in Windsor, Essex, Ontario, Canada. He married Jean Agnes Reid Maxwell, daughter of Edward Maxwell and Elizabeth Ellen Aitchison, on 10 Oct 1925 in Montréal, Montréal (Urban Agglomeration), Quebec, Canada. She was born on 02 Mar 1903 in Montréal, Montréal (Urban Agglomeration), Quebec, Canada. She died on 22 Nov 1990 in Windsor, Essex, Ontario, Canada.

viii. HUGH ERNEST FLEMING LLD was born on 11 Jun 1903 in Windsor, Essex, Ontario, Canada. He died on 30 Apr 1971 in Coburg, Northumberland, Ontario, Canada. He married Gladys Mary Cooper, daughter of William Henry Cooper and Matilda (), on 14 Mar 1941 in Amherstburg, Essex, Ontario, Canada. She was born on 15 Jul 1906 in London, England. She died on 15 Oct 1957 in Windsor, Essex, Ontario, Canada.

25.   ix.   CAROLINE BEATRICE FLEMING was born on 11 Jun 1903 in Windsor, Essex, Ontario, Canada. She died on 20 Aug 1997 in Toronto, Ontario, Canada. She married Charles Gordon Cleather, son of Edward Gordon Cleather and Ethel Lillis Scott, on 28 Jul 1927 in New York, New York, USA (Employed by Ford Motor Company). He was born on 23 Jul 1898 in Dublin, Ireland. He died on 26 May 1976 in Victoria, British Columbia, Canada.

26.   x.   BERTHA ERNESTA FLEMING was born on 08 Apr 1905 in Windsor, Essex, Ontario, Canada. She died on 09 Aug 1994 in Toronto, Ontario, Canada. She married David Steele Wright, son of David Ernest Wright and Muriel Tasker Steele, on 17 Sep 1932 in Goderich, Huron, Ontario, Canada. He was born on 13 Oct 1903 in Toronto, Ontario, Canada. He died on 05 Apr 1972 in Toronto, Ontario, Canada.

27.   xi.   JEAN HELENE FLEMING was born on 02 May 1907 in Windsor, Essex, Ontario, Canada. She died on 08 Sep 1991 in Ottawa, Ontario, Canada. She married Philip Norcross Gross Sr, son of Henry Joseph Gross and Alice Whitney, on 30 Jun 1928 in Goderich, Huron, Ontario, Canada (in summer residence of Ernest Fleming). He was born on 01 Jul 1901 in Worcester, Massachusetts, USA. He died on 03 Mar 1988 in Ottawa, Ontario, Canada.

8.   **HARWOOD ONTARIO OSBORNE**[3] **FLEMING** (Samuel[2], Daniel[1]) was born on 15 Nov 1862 in Milton, Halton, Ontario, Canada. He died on 02 Jun 1937 in Riverside, Riverside, California, USA. He married (1) **JANET GRAHAM CAMPBELL**, daughter of George Campbell and Fanny Hannah Campbell, on 11 Feb 1896 in 237 London St, Windsor, Essex, Ontario, Canada. She was born on 25 Apr 1871 in Windsor, Essex, Ontario, Canada. She died on 28 Dec 1953 in Riverside, Yolo, California, USA.

Harwood Ontario Osborne Fleming had the following children:

28.   i.   ERROL KEITH[4] FLEMING was born on 02 Apr 1897 in Sandwich, Essex, Ontario, Canada. He died on 24 Nov 1976 in Del Mar, San Diego, California, USA. He married Gwendolyn Irving Mylne, daughter of John Malloch Mylne and Elizabeth Brow Irving, on 02 Nov 1928 in Riverside, Riverside, California, USA. She was born on 11 Apr 1900 in Riverside, Riverside, California, USA. She died on 12 Nov 1996 in Del Mar, San Diego, California, USA.

     ii.   KEITH CYRUS FLEMING was born on 13 Jun 1900 in Sandwich, Essex, Ontario, Canada. He died on 01 Oct 1901 in Essex, Ontario, Canada (Cause of Death: Amenia).

     iii.   LORNA CLARA FLEMING was born on 18 Feb 1905 in Sandwich, Essex, Ontario, Canada. She died on 09 Feb 1908 in Windsor, Essex, Ontario, Canada (Cause of Death: Empyaema Following Pneumonia Heart Failure).

29.   iv.   ALEXANDER PATRICK CAMPBELL FLEMING was born on 13 Jun 1908 in Sandwich, Essex, Ontario, Canada. He died on 29 Jun 1983 in Encinitas, San Diego, California, USA. He married (1) HELEN JEAN NICHOLSON on 22 Mar 1930 in Santa Barbara, Santa Barbara, California, USA. She was born on 30 Apr 1909 in Santa Barbara, Santa Barbara, California, USA. He married (2) CLARA LOIS HUNTER, daughter of Lemna Joseph Hunter and Flora Hulda Knoll, on 05 Jul 1973 in San Diego, San Diego, California, USA. She was born on 29 Oct 1915 in Santa Cruz, Santa Cruz, California, USA. She died on 15 Jun 2006 in Cardiff-by-the-Sea, San Diego, California, USA.

Harwood Ontario Osborne Fleming and Janet Graham Campbell had the following children:

28.   i.   ERROL KEITH[4] FLEMING was born on 02 Apr 1897 in Sandwich, Essex, Ontario, Canada. He died on 24 Nov 1976 in Del Mar, San Diego, California, USA. He married Gwendolyn Irving Mylne, daughter of John Malloch Mylne and Elizabeth Brow Irving, on 02 Nov 1928 in Riverside, Riverside, California, USA. She was born on 11 Apr 1900 in Riverside, Riverside, California, USA. She died on 12 Nov 1996 in Del Mar, San Diego, California, USA.

     ii.   KEITH CYRUS FLEMING was born on 13 Jun 1900 in Sandwich, Essex, Ontario, Canada. He died on 01 Oct 1901 in Essex, Ontario, Canada (Cause of Death: Amenia).

iii. LORNA CLARA FLEMING was born on 18 Feb 1905 in Sandwich, Essex, Ontario, Canada. She died on 09 Feb 1908 in Windsor, Essex, Ontario, Canada (Cause of Death: Empyaema Following Pneumonia Heart Failure).

29. iv. ALEXANDER PATRICK CAMPBELL FLEMING was born on 13 Jun 1908 in Sandwich, Essex, Ontario, Canada. He died on 29 Jun 1983 in Encinitas, San Diego, California, USA. He married (1) HELEN JEAN NICHOLSON on 22 Mar 1930 in Santa Barbara, Santa Barbara, California, USA. She was born on 30 Apr 1909 in Santa Barbara, Santa Barbara, California, USA. He married (2) CLARA LOIS HUNTER, daughter of Lemna Joseph Hunter and Flora Hulda Knoll, on 05 Jul 1973 in San Diego, San Diego, California, USA. She was born on 29 Oct 1915 in Santa Cruz, Santa Cruz, California, USA. She died on 15 Jun 2006 in Cardiff-by-the-Sea, San Diego, California, USA.

9. **CLARENCE URIEL SIMCOE BRONTE**[3] **FLEMING** (Samuel[2], Daniel[1]) was born on 21 Aug 1866 in Bronte, Canada West, Canada. He died on 17 Nov 1941 in Pasadena, Los Angeles, California, USA. He married Mabel Rogers Taylor, daughter of Frank Dwight Taylor and Phebe Elizabeth Shords, on 08 Nov 1900 in Detroit, Wayne, Michigan, USA. She was born on 15 Dec 1873 in Detroit, Wayne, Michigan, USA. She died on 20 Jul 1941 in 224 Oak Lawn Av, Pasadena, Los Angeles, California, USA.

Clarence Uriel Simcoe Bronte Fleming and Mabel Rogers Taylor had the following child:

30. i. AUDREY RUTH[4] FLEMING was born on 05 Aug 1901 in Detroit, Wayne, Michigan, USA. She died on 03 Feb 1975 in 622 E Lake Rd, Hammondsport, Steuben, New York, USA. She married Guy Simmons Shoemaker, son of Floyd Monroe Shoemaker and Flora Lois Holmes, on 17 Apr 1923 in Pasadena, Los Angeles, California, USA. He was born on 04 Dec 1898 in Elmira, Chemung, New York, USA. He died on 09 Jul 1978 in Hammondsport, Steuben, New York, USA.

10. **SARAH FELICIA LOUISA PELL**[3] **FLEMING** (Samuel[2], Daniel[1]) was born on 16 Sep 1867 in Bronte, Halton, Ontario, Canada. She died on 26 Jun 1928 in Toronto, Ontario, Canada. She married (2) **RICHARD HURON HOLMES**, son of Thomas Holmes LLD and Elizabeth Lane, on 15 Nov 1887 in Windsor, Essex, Ontario, Canada. He was born on 06 Mar 1856 in Toronto, Ontario, Canada. He died on 05 Oct 1933 in Toronto, Ontario, Canada.

Sarah Felicia Louisa Pell Fleming had the following children:

31. i. VERA ALOHA[4] HOLMES was born on 10 Aug 1889 in Toronto, Ontario, Canada. She died on 02 Sep 1975 in Toronto, Ontario, Canada. She married Archibald William Forbes DDS, son of William Forbes and Elizabeth Forbes, on 25 Dec 1912 in Old St. Andrew's Church, Toronto, Ontario, Canada. He was born on 01 Nov 1876 in Elma, Perth, Ontario, Canada. He died on 08 Mar 1942 in Toronto, Ontario, Canada (Cause o Death: Myocardistis - high blood pressure).

32. ii. JOHN GUMSER HOLMES was born on 28 Sep 1890 in Toronto, Ontario, Canada. He died on 06 Jun 1953 in Toronto, Ontario, Canada. He married (1) SARAH ETHEL CHATTERSON. She was born on 10 Apr 1917 in Toronto, Ontario, Canada (Father: James Walter Chatterson (1890-1953) / Mother: Mary A Lees (1895-1963)). She died on 19 Dec 2003 in Shelburne, Dufferin, Ontario, Canada. He married (2) IRENE MYRTLE DYNES MACKINTOSH, daughter of John Argyll Macintosh and Rachel Ann Agnes Dynes Dewar Macintosh, in 1914. She was born on 05 Sep 1894 in Dufftown, Banffshire, Scotland. She died on 25 May 1993.

iii. GOLU LILLA HOLMES was born on 13 Feb 1893 in Toronto, Ontario, Canada. She died on 26 Dec 1963 in 63 Forbes St, Victoria, British Columbia, Canada. She married Graham Frederick Simmonds, son of Herbert Henry Simmonds and Louisa Ada Gould, on 05 Jan 1918 in Toronto, Ontario, Canada. He was born about 1892 in Isle of Wight, England. He died on 15 Jan 1974 in Victoria, British Columbia, Canada.

33. iv. THOMAS BYRON HOLMES was born on 10 Aug 1895 in York, Ontario, Canada. He died on 20 Aug 1979 in Toronto, Ontario, Canada (Cause of Death: Pneumionia). He married (1) IRMA MARGARET MARTIN, daughter of Edward

Daniel Martin and Agnes Jane Perry, on 21 May 1924 in Winnipeg, Manitoba, Canada. She was born on 13 Sep 1896 in Manitoba, Canada. She died on 28 Nov 1989 in Toronto, Ontario, Canada. He married an unknown spouse on 21 May 1924 in Winnipeg, Manitoba, Canada.

34.   v.   OLGA EVELYN WENOWAE HOLMES was born on 10 May 1897 in Toronto, Ontario, Canada. She died on 02 Mar 1942 in (Likely), Toronto, Ontario, Canada. She married Russell McGill, son of William Robert McGill and Ann Eversfield, on 03 Sep 1918 in Halton, Ontario, Canada. He was born on 27 Mar 1894 in Toronto, Ontario, Canada. He died on 26 Feb 1927 in York, Ontario, Canada.

        vi.   ELIZA FELICIA FLEMING HOLMES was born on 24 Mar 1900 in Toronto, Ontario, Canada. She died in 1997. She married (1) WILFRED BYATT ANASTARIUS IZZARD, son of William George Izzard and Harriet Craven Buckley, on 11 Oct 1923 in York, Ontario, Canada. He was born on 17 Dec 1898 in Toronto, Ontario, Canada (Father: William George Izzard (1846-) / Mother: Harriet Craven Buckley (1864-)). She married an unknown spouse on 11 Oct 1923 in York, Ontario, Canada.

35.   vii.   HERALD RICHARD HOLMES was born on 12 Oct 1905 in Huron, Ontario, Canada. He died on 03 Oct 1974 in Guelph, Wellington, Ontario, Canada. He married (1) EHRMA I DEGUERRE on 24 Aug 1935 in Buffalo, Erie, New York, USA. She was born on 23 Apr 1908 in Toronto, Ontario, Canada. She died in 1989.

Richard Huron Holmes and Sarah Felicia Louisa Pell Fleming had the following children:

31.   i.   VERA ALOHA[4] HOLMES was born on 10 Aug 1889 in Toronto, Ontario, Canada. She died on 02 Sep 1975 in Toronto, Ontario, Canada. She married Archibald William Forbes DDS, son of William Forbes and Elizabeth Forbes, on 25 Dec 1912 in Old St. Andrew's Church, Toronto, Ontario, Canada. He was born on 01 Nov 1876 in Elma, Perth, Ontario, Canada. He died on 08 Mar 1942 in Toronto, Ontario, Canada (Cause o Death: Myocardistis - high blood pressure).

32.   ii.   JOHN GUMSER HOLMES was born on 28 Sep 1890 in Toronto, Ontario, Canada. He died on 06 Jun 1953 in Toronto, Ontario, Canada. He married (1) SARAH ETHEL CHATTERSON. She was born on 10 Apr 1917 in Toronto, Ontario, Canada (Father: James Walter Chatterson (1890-1953) / Mother: Mary A Lees (1895-1963)). She died on 19 Dec 2003 in Shelburne, Dufferin, Ontario, Canada. He married (2) IRENE MYRTLE DYNES MACKINTOSH, daughter of John Argyll Macintosh and Rachel Ann Agnes Dynes Dewar Macintosh, in 1914. She was born on 05 Sep 1894 in Dufftown, Banffshire, Scotland. She died on 25 May 1993.

        iii.   GOLU LILLA HOLMES was born on 13 Feb 1893 in Toronto, Ontario, Canada. She died on 26 Dec 1963 in 63 Forbes St, Victoria, British Columbia, Canada. She married Graham Frederick Simmonds, son of Herbert Henry Simmonds and Louisa Ada Gould, on 05 Jan 1918 in Toronto, Ontario, Canada. He was born about 1892 in Isle of Wight, England. He died on 15 Jan 1974 in Victoria, British Columbia, Canada.

33.   iv.   THOMAS BYRON HOLMES was born on 10 Aug 1895 in York, Ontario, Canada. He died on 20 Aug 1979 in Toronto, Ontario, Canada (Cause of Death: Pneumionia). He married (1) IRMA MARGARET MARTIN, daughter of Edward Daniel Martin and Agnes Jane Perry, on 21 May 1924 in Winnipeg, Manitoba, Canada. She was born on 13 Sep 1896 in Manitoba, Canada. She died on 28 Nov 1989 in Toronto, Ontario, Canada. He married an unknown spouse on 21 May 1924 in Winnipeg, Manitoba, Canada.

34.   v.   OLGA EVELYN WENOWAE HOLMES was born on 10 May 1897 in Toronto, Ontario, Canada. She died on 02 Mar 1942 in (Likely), Toronto, Ontario, Canada. She married Russell McGill, son of William Robert McGill and Ann Eversfield, on 03 Sep 1918 in Halton, Ontario, Canada. He was born on 27

Mar 1894 in Toronto, Ontario, Canada. He died on 26 Feb 1927 in York, Ontario, Canada.

vi. ELIZA FELICIA FLEMING HOLMES was born on 24 Mar 1900 in Toronto, Ontario, Canada. She died in 1997. She married (1) WILFRED BYATT ANASTARIUS IZZARD, son of William George Izzard and Harriet Craven Buckley, on 11 Oct 1923 in York, Ontario, Canada. He was born on 17 Dec 1898 in Toronto, Ontario, Canada (Father: William George Izzard (1846-) / Mother: Harriet Craven Buckley (1864-)). She married an unknown spouse on 11 Oct 1923 in York, Ontario, Canada.

35.   vii. HERALD RICHARD HOLMES was born on 12 Oct 1905 in Huron, Ontario, Canada. He died on 03 Oct 1974 in Guelph, Wellington, Ontario, Canada. He married (1) EHRMA I DEGUERRE on 24 Aug 1935 in Buffalo, Erie, New York, USA. She was born on 23 Apr 1908 in Toronto, Ontario, Canada. She died in 1989.

11.   **FLORENCE SELENICA VIOLA³ FLEMING** (Samuel², Daniel¹) was born on 10 Aug 1869 in Walkerville, Essex, Ontario, Canada. She died on 25 Mar 1965 in Riverside, Yolo, California, USA. She married William Everette Scotten, son of Walter Scotten and Martha E McCard, on 16 Sep 1891 in Essex, Ontario, Canada. He was born on 17 Jul 1857 in Quincy, Houghton, Michigan, USA. He died on 19 May 1945 in Pasadena, Los Angeles, California, USA.

William Everette Scotten and Florence Selenica Viola Fleming had the following children:

i. SIDNEY TEMPLE⁴ SCOTTEN was born on 03 May 1901 in Detroit, Wayne, Michigan, USA. He died on 10 May 1901 in Detroit, Wayne, Michigan, USA.

36.   ii. WILLIAM EVERETTE SCOTTEN JR was born on 24 Aug 1904 in Detroit, Wayne, Michigan, USA. He died on 27 Nov 1958 in Orange, California, USA. He married Caroline Cornelia Tarcea, daughter of Dumitru Dan Tarcea and Maria Fritea, on 01 May 1943 in District of Columbia, USA. She was born on 21 Jun 1917 in Akron, Summit, Ohio, USA. She died on 02 Apr 2003 in La Habra, Orange, California, USA.

iii. ARTHUR FLEMING SCOTTEN was born on 01 Aug 1907 in Rochester, Oakland, Michigan, USA. He died on 19 Nov 1992 in San Diego, California, USA.

12.   **JASPER F³ MARTIN** (Mary Ann² Fleming, Daniel¹ Fleming) was born on 22 Jun 1854 in Milton, Halton, Canada West, Canada. He died on 09 Mar 1892 in Ypsilanti, Washtenaw, Michigan, USA (M T Conklin home, Congress & Summit Sts,). He married Eva E Rogers, daughter of Oscar K Rogers and Margaret L Cook, on 09 Sep 1879 in Washtenaw, Michigan, USA. She was born in 1859 in Ypsilanti, Washtenaw, Michigan, USA.

Jasper F Martin and Eva E Rogers had the following children:

37.   i. JOSEPH LACY⁴ MARTIN was born on 02 May 1880 in Ypsilanti, Washtenaw, Michigan, USA. He died on 13 Feb 1968 in Ventura, California, USA. He married (1) ALMA EMMA ANDERSON, daughter of Marinus Andersen and Susan Nielson, on 01 Dec 1937 in Fort Dodge, Webster, Iowa, USA. She was born on 27 Jun 1909 in Palmer, Merrick, Nebraska, USA. She died on 08 Mar 1998 in Tempe, Maricopa, Arizona, USA. He married (2) HARRIET JANE COOK, daughter of Charles Henry Cook and Sabra Ann Russell, on 21 Jun 1909 in Le Mars, Plymouth, Iowa, USA. She was born about 1888 in Vermillion, Clay, South Dakota, USA. She died on 11 Jan 1976 in Escondido, San Diego, California, USA.

ii. ALBERT EDWARD MARTIN was born on 01 Mar 1882 in St Louis, Gratiot, Michigan, USA. He died on 28 Apr 1960 in Hennepin, Minnesota, USA. He married Renata L Guse, daughter of Herman H Guse and Helene Auguste Henke, in 1911. She was born on 07 May 1888 in Watertown, Jefferson, Wisconsin, USA. She died on 28 Sep 1965 in Hennepin, Minnesota, USA.

iii. EVA LYNNE MARTIN was born on 07 Jul 1884 in Ypsilanti, Washtenaw, Michigan, USA. She died on 26 Apr 1969 in St Petersburg, Pinellas, Florida, USA. She married (1) JOHN CHARLES HARRIS, son of George W Harris and Mary Baker, on 22 Apr 1907 in Council Bluffs, Pottawattamie, Iowa, USA. He was born on 18 Jul 1878 in Chicago, Cook, Illinois, USA. She married (2) JAMES TEMPLETON LIBBEY. He was born on 17 Jun 1879 in Liverpool, Columbiana, Ohio, USA. He died on 02 Aug 1972 in Pinellas, Florida, USA.

13. **EDWARD DANIEL**[3] **MARTIN** (Mary Ann[2] Fleming, Daniel[1] Fleming) was born on 30 Sep 1856 in Milton, Halton, Canada West, Canada. He died on 14 May 1938 in Toronto, Ontario, Canada. He married Agnes Jane Perry, daughter of James Perry and Agnes Nancy Kerr, on 06 Aug 1879 in Ottawa, Ontario, Canada. She was born in May 1860 in Ottawa, Ontario, Canada. She died on 10 Dec 1945 in Forest Hill, Toronto, Ontario, Canada (Cause of Death: Old age).

Edward Daniel Martin and Agnes Jane Perry had the following children:

        i.   MABEL AGNES[4] MARTIN was born on 11 Jul 1880 in Carleton, Ontario, Canada. She died on 26 Jul 1881 in Carleton, Ontario, Canada (Cause of Death: Diarrhea).

38.   ii.   ELIZABETH PERRY MARTIN was born on 14 Jul 1882 in Carleton, Ontario, Canada. She died in 1962 in Toronto, Ontario, Canada. She married Albert Courtney Gillespie, son of George Edward Gillespie and Mary Meudell, in 1903. He was born on 10 Nov 1877 in Toronto, Ontario, Canada. He died on 09 May 1943 in Toronto, Ontario, Canada.

        iii.   EDWARD WATSON MARTIN was born on 30 Dec 1884 in Ottawa, Ontario, Canada. He died in 1975 in Victoria, British Columbia, Canada (Occupation: Manager, Drug Company). He married Gladys Louisa Brock, daughter of Jeffrey Hall Brook and Louisa Adelaide Clara Gillespie, on 13 Jun 1909 in Winnipeg, Manitoba, Canada. She was born on 23 Jun 1889 in Winnipeg, Manitoba, Canada. She died on 24 Oct 1986 in Victoria, British Columbia, Canada.

39.   iv.   JEAN AGNES MARTIN was born on 22 Jul 1886 in Carleton, Ontario, Canada. She died on 14 Dec 1957 in Ontario, Canada. She married Daniel Campbell MacLachlan, son of Alexander Campbell MacLachlan and Jane Garson, on 08 Oct 1912 in Winnipeg, Manitoba, Canada. He was born on 15 Oct 1882 in Guelph, Wellington, Ontario, Canada. He died on 27 Apr 1964 in Toronto, Ontario, Canada.

        v.   MARGARET MARY MARTIN was born on 12 Sep 1890 in Winnipeg, Manitoba, Canada. She died on 09 Jul 1939 in 105 Old Forest Hill Rd, Toronto, Ontario, Canada (Cause of death: heart failure following 15 yrs with heart disease.).

40.   vi.   MARY FLEMING MARTIN was born on 21 May 1894 in Winnipeg, Manitoba, Canada. She died on 12 May 1991 in Vancouver, British Columbia, Canada. She married Kenneth Gordon Nairn, son of John Nairn Jr and Amy Gertrude Rides, on 16 Dec 1920 in Winnipeg, Manitoba, Canada. He was born on 09 Nov 1898 in Edinburgh Newington, Midlothian, Scotland. He died on 29 Oct 1988 in Vancouver, British Columbia, Canada (Death year cited in wife's obituary.).

41.   vii.   IRMA MARGARET MARTIN was born on 13 Sep 1896 in Manitoba, Canada. She died on 28 Nov 1989 in Toronto, Ontario, Canada. She married (2) THOMAS BYRON HOLMES, son of Richard Huron Holmes and Sarah Felicia Louisa Pell Fleming, on 21 May 1924 in Winnipeg, Manitoba, Canada. He was born on 10 Aug 1895 in York, Ontario, Canada. He died on 20 Aug 1979 in Toronto, Ontario, Canada (Cause of Death: Pneumionia).

        viii.   JACK FOSTER MARTIN was born on 24 Dec 1898 in Ontario, Canada. He died in 1912 in (Likely), Winnipeg, Manitoba, Canada.

14. **MARY A**[3] **MARTIN** (Mary Ann[2] Fleming, Daniel[1] Fleming) was born on 23 Sep 1865 in Ypsilanti, Washtenaw, Michigan, USA. She died on 19 Dec 1946 in San Diego, California, USA. She married Jerome W Robbins on 31 Jul 1897 in Lucas, Ohio, USA.

Jerome W Robbins and Mary A Martin had the following child:

        i.   HAZEL MAY[4] ROBBINS was born on 19 Jul 1894 in Sandusky, Erie, Ohio, USA. She died on 24 Jan 1978 in San Diego, California, USA.

15. **EMMA KEELER** (Lucy A[2] Fleming, Daniel[1] Fleming) was born on 09 Aug 1865 in Olathe, Johnson, Kansas, USA. She died on 06 Apr 1953. She married George T Emslie on 27 Oct 1884 in Johnson, Kansas, USA. He was born about 1853 in England. He died in 1900.

George T Emslie and Emma Keeler had the following children:

    i.   EMMETT KEELER EMSLIE was born on 01 Aug 1887 in Colorado, USA. He died in Aug 1967.

    ii.   KATHERINE LUCY EMSLIE was born in Jun 1889 in Colorado, USA. She died on 19 Nov 1976.

    iii.   RALPH EMSLIE was born on 26 Aug 1893 in Wakefield, Clay, Kansas, USA. He died in 1984.

16.   **JULIA AUGUSTA KEELER** (Lucy A[2] Fleming, Daniel[1] Fleming) was born on 12 Jan 1869 in Olathe, Johnson, Kansas, USA. She died on 04 Oct 1944. She married John Alex Logan Boyd, son of Marshall Wesley Boyd and Minerva Richards, in 1884. He was born on 14 Oct 1865 in Creal Springs, Williamson, Illinois, USA. He died on 15 Oct 1942 in Springfield, Greene, Missouri, USA.

John Alex Logan Boyd and Julia Augusta Keeler had the following children:

    i.   HARRY L BOYD was born in 1894 in Kansas, USA.

    ii.   LUCY ORA BOYD was born on 05 Sep 1895 in Rosedale, Wyandotte, Kansas, USA. She died in Mar 1978 in Springfield, Greene, Missouri, USA.

    iii.   EARL JULIUS BOYD was born on 21 Sep 1897 in Kansas City, Wyandotte, Kansas, USA. He died on 06 Jan 1971 in Springfield, Greene, Missouri, USA.

    iv.   JOHN THOMAS BOYD was born on 18 Oct 1899 in Kansas City, Wyandotte, Kansas, USA. He died in 1968 in Springfield, Greene, Missouri, USA.

    v.   WALTER BOYD was born in 1902 in Missouri, USA.

    vi.   ALICE M BOYD was born on 02 Feb 1908 in Kansas City, Jackson, Missouri, USA.

17.   **LEWIS[3] KEELER** (Lucy A[2] Fleming, Daniel[1] Fleming) was born on 20 Aug 1870 in Olathe, Johnson, Kansas, USA. He died on 22 Jun 1953 in Garden City, Finney, Kansas, USA. He married Sadie Inez Davis, daughter of Roderick Ransom Davis and Nancy Sarah Aumiller, in Jan 1895 in Gray County, Kansas, USA. She was born on 08 Sep 1872 in Greenwood, Franklin, Kansas, USA. She died on 17 Aug 1956 in 5011 Pleasant St, Polk, Iowa, USA (died at home of daughter).

Lewis Keeler and Sadie Inez Davis had the following children:

    i.   JULIA ANNETTE[4] KEELER was born on 04 Nov 1895 in Hays, Ellis, Kansas, USA. She died on 10 Dec 1990 in Polk, Iowa, USA.

    ii.   LEWIS R KEELER was born in Apr 1897 in Garden City, Finney, Kansas, USA. He died on 25 Aug 1902 in Garden City, Finney, Kansas, USA.

18.   **ANNA DAVENPORT[3] KEELER** (Lucy A[2] Fleming, Daniel[1] Fleming) was born on 03 Dec 1872 in Olathe, Johnson, Kansas, USA. She died on 08 Sep 1957 in Lawrence, Douglas, Kansas, USA. She married Harry Burton White, son of Thomas King White and Sarah Ann Elizabeth Little, on 31 Dec 1895 in Wakefield, Clay, Kansas, USA. He was born on 11 Feb 1872 in Wakefield, Clay, Kansas, USA. He died on 19 Aug 1909 in Wakefield, Clay, Kansas, USA (Madura Cemetery, Wakefield, Clay County, Kansas, USA).

Harry Burton White and Anna Davenport Keeler had the following children:

    i.   EDNA LEONA[4] WHITE was born on 07 Jan 1897 in Wakefield, Clay, Kansas, USA. She died on 06 Apr 1975 in Peridot, Gila, Arizona, USA.

    ii.   MARY THELMA WHITE was born on 03 Oct 1898 in Wakefield, Clay, Kansas, USA. She died on 11 Feb 1902 in Wakefield, Clay, Kansas, USA.

    iii.   THEODORE KEELER WHITE was born on 05 Jun 1900 in Wakefield, Clay, Kansas, USA. He died on 16 Feb 1902 in Wakefield, Clay, Kansas, USA.

42.   iv.   ANNA JOYCE WHITE was born on 30 Jul 1902 in Wakefield, Clay, Kansas, USA. She died on 30 Jan 1992 in Phoenix, Maricopa, Arizona, USA. She married Harvey Cyrus Osborne LLD, son of Fred Osborne and Emma Louise Paul, on 20 Oct 1929 in 1207 East Franklin Apt E, Lawrence, Douglas, Kansas, USA. He was born on 07 Oct 1898 in Ashland, Clark, Kansas, USA. He died on 21 Oct 1967 in Globe, Gila,

Arizona, USA.

<table>
<tr><td>v.</td><td>HAROLD BERT WHITE was born on 25 Dec 1903 in Wakefield, Clay, Kansas, USA. He died on 29 Nov 1985 in Lawrence, Douglas, Kansas, USA. He married Wilma Frances Bump, daughter of George Franklin Bump and Frances Elizabeth Williams, on 14 Sep 1940 in Lawrence, Douglas, Kansas, USA. She was born on 14 Sep 1908 in Phillipsburg, Phillips, Kansas, USA. She died on 31 Mar 1972 in Lawrence, Douglas, Kansas, USA.</td></tr>
</table>

43.   vi.   LEWIS BURTON WHITE was born on 12 May 1906 in Wakefield, Clay, Kansas, USA (Father: Burton White / Mother: Ann D). He died in Jul 1982 in Topeka, Shawnee, Kansas, USA (Cause of Death: Heart Attack). He married Marion Adelle Fletcher, daughter of Burton Raymond Fletcher and Elsie Victoria Boutwell, on 05 Apr 1930 in Lawrence, Douglas, Kansas, USA. She was born on 15 Jan 1913 in Nebraska, USA. She died on 14 Feb 1983 in Topeka, Shawnee, Kansas, USA (Topeka Hospital).

vii.   LAURENCE KEELER WHITE was born on 17 Jul 1908 in Wakefield, Clay, Kansas, USA. He died on 04 May 1973 in Globe, Gila, Arizona, USA.

Generation 4

19.   **MARJORIE⁴ FLEMING** (Arthur Samuel Henry³, Samuel², Daniel¹) was born on 14 Oct 1894 in Detroit, Wayne, Michigan, USA. She died on 11 Apr 1985 in Palm Beach, Florida, USA. She married (1) **WILTON LLOYD-SMITH**, son of Walter Lloyd-Smith and Jessie E Gonzales, on 25 Aug 1917 in Pasadena, Los Angeles, California, USA. He was born on 24 May 1894 in Elmira Heights, Elmira, Chemung, New York, USA. He died on 29 Feb 1940 in Manhattan, New York, New York, USA (committed suicide.). She married (2) **KNIGHT WOOLLEY**. He was born on 01 May 1895 in Brooklyn, Kings, New York, USA. He died on 18 Jan 1984 in Hobe Sound, Martin, Florida, USA.

Wilton Lloyd-Smith and Marjorie Fleming had the following children:

44.   i.   MARJORIE⁵ LLOYD-SMITH was born on 18 Jul 1918 in New York, New York, USA. She died on 30 Mar 2004 in Washington, District of Columbia, USA. She married (1) GEORGE MARSHALL HORNBLOWER, son of George Sanford Hornblower and Dorothy Marshall, on 10 Nov 1940 in Elmira, Chemung, New York, USA. He was born on 19 Nov 1917 in New York, New York, USA (Father: George Sanford Hornblower (1884-) / Mother: Dorothy Marshall (1886-1968)). He died on 06 Oct 2006 in Washington, District of Columbia, USA.

ii.   JOSEPHINE LLOYD-SMITH was born on 19 Sep 1920 in New York, New York, USA. She died on 14 Mar 1925 in New York, New York, USA.

iii.   CLARA F LLOYD-SMITH was born on 28 Nov 1921 in New York, New York, USA. She died in 1984 in New York, New York, USA.

iv.   VIRGINIA LLOYD-SMITH was born on 29 Oct 1925 in New York, New York, USA. She died on 13 Jan 2006 in New Mexico, USA.

v.   DIANE LLOYD-SMITH was born on 20 Feb 1929 in New York, New York, USA. She died after 1940.

20.   **DONALD WILLIAM⁴ FLEMING** (Oscar Ernest³ LLD, Samuel², Daniel¹) was born on 25 Mar 1892 in Windsor, Essex, Ontario, Canada. He died on 20 Oct 1961 in Riverside Manor, Windsor, Essex, Ontario, Canada. He married Isabella Mary Blanchard, daughter of Louis Blanchard and Mary Ellen Tobin, on 04 Jun 1921 in Winnipeg, Manitoba, Canada. She was born on 05 Mar 1888 in Charlottenburgh, Glengarry, Ontario, Canada (Father: Louis Blanchard (1828-1903) / Mother: Mary Ellen Tobin (1842-1929)). She died on 07 Jul 1951 in Cantley, Les Collines-de-l'Outaouais, Quebec, Canada.

Donald William Fleming and Isabella Mary Blanchard had the following children:

i.   HELEN JOAN⁵ FLEMING was born on 19 Jun 1922 in Calgary, Alberta, Canada. She died on 06 Mar 2012 in Toronto, Ontario, Canada.

ii.   DONALD WIGTON FLEMING was born on 26 Jun 1927 in Sandwich, Essex, Ontario, Canada. He died on 17 Jan 1928 in Essex, Ontario, Canada (Cause of Death: Pneumonia Meningitis).

21.   FRANCES MAUD⁴ FLEMING (Oscar Ernest³ LLD, Samuel², Daniel¹) was born on 08 Jan 1894 in Windsor, Essex, Ontario, Canada. She died on 21 Aug 1980 in Ottawa, Ontario, Canada. She married Harold George Kerrigan, son of James Kerrigan and Augusta Bryson Moore, on 18 Dec 1915 in Sandwich St W, Windsor, Essex, Ontario, Canada. He was born on 02 Jun 1879 in Toronto, Ontario, Canada. He died on 17 Feb 1928 in Los Angeles, California, USA.

Harold George Kerrigan and Frances Maud Fleming had the following children:

45.   i.   HAROLD FLEMING⁵ KERRIGAN was born on 10 Jun 1917 in Sandwich, Essex, Ontario, Canada. He died on 03 Sep 1993 in Knowlton, Brome-Missisquoi, Quebec, Canada. He married (1) VIRGINIA ERNESTINE PORTER, daughter of Ernest Albee Porter and Emma Bernice Porter, on 12 Aug 1944 in Brookline, Norfolk, Massachusetts, USA. She was born in 1922 in Brookline, Norfolk, Massachusetts, USA. He married an unknown spouse in 1944 in Brookline, Norfolk, Massachusetts, USA.

46.   ii.   PETER FREDERICK KERRIGAN was born on 24 Mar 1919 in Walkerville, Essex, Ontario, Canada. He died on 01 Jun 1992 in Knowlton, Brome-Missisquoi, Quebec, Canada. He married Margaret Claire Fisher, daughter of Philip Sydney Fisher and Margaret Southam, on 15 May 1946 in Montréal, Montréal (Urban Agglomeration), Quebec, Canada. She was born about 1924 in (Likely), Montréal, Montréal (Urban Agglomeration), Quebec, Canada.

47.   iii.   BARBARA FRANCES KERRIGAN was born on 04 Jul 1920 in Walkerville, Essex, Ontario, Canada. She died on 21 May 2007 in Ottawa, Ontario, Canada. She married William Donald Munro Sr, son of William Munro and Ethel Hall, on 06 Jul 1953 in Montréal, Montréal (Urban Agglomeration), Quebec, Canada. He was born on 29 Mar 1922 in Titusville, Crawford, Pennsylvania, USA. He died on 28 Feb 2007 in Ottawa, Ontario, Canada.

48.   iv.   GEOFFREY MOORE KERRIGAN was born on 06 Nov 1921 in London, Middlesex, Ontario, Canada. He died on 21 Feb 2013 in Middlesex Hospice, Middlesex, Connecticut, USA. He married Marjorie Brooks, daughter of Harry Brooks and Mary Hannah Lavender, on 25 Mar 1943 in Cleveland, Yorkshire, England. She was born on 12 Sep 1921 in Ormesby, Yorkshire, England. She died on 13 May 2009 in Essex, Middlesex, Connecticut, USA.

49.   v.   JOCELYN ANN KERRIGAN was born on 25 Sep 1926 in Goderich, Huron, Ontario, Canada. She died on 11 Feb 1995 in Ottawa, Ontario, Canada (Cause of Death: cancer). She married Robin Benitz on 02 May 1959 in Montréal, Montréal (Urban Agglomeration), Quebec, Canada (Personal notes --> https://www.ancestry.ca/family-tree/person/tree/111982665/person/370093036050/facts). He was born about 1925.

22.   OSCAR EDWARD SCOTTEN⁴ FLEMING LLD (Oscar Ernest³ LLD, Samuel², Daniel¹) was born on 13 Feb 1897 in Windsor, Essex, Ontario, Canada. He died on 03 Jan 1957 in London, Middlesex, Ontario, Canada. He married (1) IRENE FAIRCLOUGH on 28 Jul 1927 in Windsor, Essex, Ontario, Canada. She was born about 1906 in Barnsley, Shropshire, England. She died in 1990. He married (2) JULIA ANTOINETTE CHANEL, daughter of Albert Chanel and Jeanne Eugenie DeVolle, on 11 Nov 1919 in Paris, Île-de-France, France. She was born on 13 Jun 1887 in Issoire, Puy-de-Dôme, Auvergne, France. She died on 02 May 1921 in Buenos Aires, Argentina.

Oscar Edward Scotten Fleming LLD and Irene Fairclough had the following child:

i.   MARY AUGUSTA⁵ FLEMING was born about 1949 in (Likely), Windsor, Essex, Ontario, Canada. She married Walter Osgood Sherman Lake about 1969 in Charlotte, St Vincent and the Grenadines.

23. **CANMORE DRAKE**[4] **FLEMING** (Oscar Ernest[3] LLD, Samuel[2], Daniel[1]) was born on 02 Jan 1899 in Windsor, Essex, Ontario, Canada. He died on 08 Feb 1967 in Etobicoke, Toronto, Ontario, Canada. He married Evelyn Eileen Johnston, daughter of Arthur James Johnston and Amy Eliza Mason, on 23 May 1944 in Toronto, Ontario, Canada. She was born on 29 Dec 1903 in Toronto, Ontario, Canada. She died on 21 Feb 1976 in Toronto, Ontario, Canada.

    Canmore Drake Fleming and Evelyn Eileen Johnston had the following child:

        i.   PETER[5] FLEMING was born about 1946 in (Likely), Islington, Toronto, Ontario, Canada.

24. **KENNETH ELDON**[4] **FLEMING** (Oscar Ernest[3] LLD, Samuel[2], Daniel[1]) was born on 07 Nov 1900 in Windsor, Essex, Ontario, Canada. He died on 05 Oct 1965 in Windsor, Essex, Ontario, Canada. He married Jean Agnes Reid Maxwell, daughter of Edward Maxwell and Elizabeth Ellen Aitchison, on 10 Oct 1925 in Montréal, Montréal (Urban Agglomeration), Quebec, Canada. She was born on 02 Mar 1903 in Montréal, Montréal (Urban Agglomeration), Quebec, Canada. She died on 22 Nov 1990 in Windsor, Essex, Ontario, Canada.

    Kenneth Eldon Fleming and Jean Agnes Reid Maxwell had the following child:

    50.   i.   JEAN ELIZABETH[5] FLEMING was born on 02 Mar 1927 in Montréal, Montréal (Urban Agglomeration), Quebec, Canada. She died on 24 Nov 2008 in Greenwich, Fairfield, Connecticut, USA. She married (1) SYDNEY ANGLIN WOODD-CAHUSAC REV, son of Kenneth Anglin Woodd-Cahusac and Beatrice Maude Barry, on 01 Dec 1951 in Niagara St, Riverside, Missaukee, Michigan, USA. He was born on 02 Apr 1918 in New York, New York, USA. He died on 03 Jan 2004 in Greenwich, Fairfield, Connecticut, USA.

25. **CAROLINE BEATRICE**[4] **FLEMING** (Oscar Ernest[3] LLD, Samuel[2], Daniel[1]) was born on 11 Jun 1903 in Windsor, Essex, Ontario, Canada. She died on 20 Aug 1997 in Toronto, Ontario, Canada. She married Charles Gordon Cleather, son of Edward Gordon Cleather and Ethel Lillis Scott, on 28 Jul 1927 in New York, New York, USA (Employed by Ford Motor Company). He was born on 23 Jul 1898 in Dublin, Ireland. He died on 26 May 1976 in Victoria, British Columbia, Canada.

    Charles Gordon Cleather and Caroline Beatrice Fleming had the following children:

    51.   i.   CATHERINE ANN GORDON[5] CLEATHER was born on 21 Jun 1928 in (Likely), New York, New York, USA. She died on 27 Mar 2017 in North York General Hospital, Toronto, Ontario, Canada. She married Joseph Louis Charles Vanderheyden on 14 Apr 1956 in Church of the Lady of the Assumption, Toronto, Ontario, Canada. He was born about 1928. He died in 2001 in Toronto, Ontario, Canada.

    52.   ii.   EDWARD GORDON CLEATHER was born on 11 Dec 1929 in St John, Saint John, New Brunswick, Canada. He died on 06 Aug 2021 in Toronto, Ontario, Canada. He married Joan Margaret Allen, daughter of W Graham Allen, on 28 Nov 1959 in Halifax, Nova Scotia, Canada. She was born about 1930 in (Likely), Windsor, Essex, Ontario, Canada. She died after 2021.

    53.   iii.   GILLIAN GORDON CLEATHER was born in Jul 1937 (Kensington, London, England). She married (1) YOUNG. He was born about 1950. She married (2) HAROLD PAUL CUSHING HAYNES. He was born in 1937.

26. **BERTHA ERNESTA**[4] **FLEMING** (Oscar Ernest[3] LLD, Samuel[2], Daniel[1]) was born on 08 Apr 1905 in Windsor, Essex, Ontario, Canada. She died on 09 Aug 1994 in Toronto, Ontario, Canada. She married David Steele Wright, son of David Ernest Wright and Muriel Tasker Steele, on 17 Sep 1932 in Goderich, Huron, Ontario, Canada. He was born on 13 Oct 1903 in Toronto, Ontario, Canada. He died on 05 Apr 1972 in Toronto, Ontario, Canada.

    David Steele Wright and Bertha Ernesta Fleming had the following children:

    54.   i.   DAVID FLEMING[5] WRIGHT was born about 1934 in (Likely), 10 Bridgetown Rd, Toronto, Ontario, Canada. He married Mary Ann Langmuir, daughter of Bryant Langmuir, on 09 Nov 1960 in Lewiston, Niagara, New York, USA. She was born about 1935.

ii.   LYNDY WRIGHT was born about 1935 in (Likely), 10 Bridgetown Rd, Toronto, Ontario, Canada. She married MICHAEL HEGGIE. He was born about 1935 in (Likely), Toronto, Ontario, Canada.

27.   **JEAN HELENE⁴ FLEMING** (Oscar Ernest³ LLD, Samuel², Daniel¹) was born on 02 May 1907 in Windsor, Essex, Ontario, Canada. She died on 08 Sep 1991 in Ottawa, Ontario, Canada. She married Philip Norcross Gross Sr, son of Henry Joseph Gross and Alice Whitney, on 30 Jun 1928 in Goderich, Huron, Ontario, Canada (in summer residence of Ernest Fleming). He was born on 01 Jul 1901 in Worcester, Massachusetts, USA. He died on 03 Mar 1988 in Ottawa, Ontario, Canada.

Philip Norcross Gross Sr and Jean Helene Fleming had the following children:

55.   i.   CHARLES FLEMING⁵ GROSS was born on 22 Mar 1930 in Toronto, Ontario, Canada. He died on 11 Aug 2021 in Montréal, Montréal (Urban Agglomeration), Quebec, Canada. He married Rosamond Aletha Jones, daughter of Arthur Frederick Hill Jones and Aletha Rosamond Chestnut, on 13 Feb 1954 in Oakville, Halton, Ontario, Canada. She was born on 17 Feb 1931 in Toronto, Ontario, Canada. She died on 07 Nov 2017 in Ottawa, Ontario, Canada.

56.   ii.   PHILIP NORCROSS GROSS JR was born about 1940 in (Likely), Montréal, Montréal (Urban Agglomeration), Quebec, Canada. He married Norma Jean Beattie, daughter of Norman Karl Beattie, on 29 Jun 1964 in Fredericton, York, New Brunswick, Canada. She was born in 1941 in (Likely), Montréal, Montréal (Urban Agglomeration), Quebec, Canada.

28.   **ERROL KEITH⁴ FLEMING** (Harwood Ontario Osborne³, Samuel², Daniel¹) was born on 02 Apr 1897 in Sandwich, Essex, Ontario, Canada. He died on 24 Nov 1976 in Del Mar, San Diego, California, USA. He married Gwendolyn Irving Mylne, daughter of John Malloch Mylne and Elizabeth Brow Irving, on 02 Nov 1928 in Riverside, Riverside, California, USA. She was born on 11 Apr 1900 in Riverside, Riverside, California, USA. She died on 12 Nov 1996 in Del Mar, San Diego, California, USA.

Notes for Errol Keith Fleming:

Errol Keith Fleming and Gwendolyn Irving Mylne had the following children:

i.   BABY BOY⁵ FLEMING was born on 26 Aug 1931 in Riverside, California, USA. He died on 26 Aug 1931 in Riverside, California, USA.

ii.   ERROL IAN FLEMING was born on 06 May 1933 in Riverside, Riverside, California, USA. He died on 30 Sep 1952 in Riverside, Riverside, California, USA (in swimming pool at Riverside YWCA (now the Art Center)).

iii.   NOEL I FLEMING was born on 13 Nov 1935 in Riverside, California, USA. He married Marilyn Gayle () in 1985. She was born in 1940 in Riverside, California, USA. She died on 15 Jan 2020 in Del Mar, San Diego, California, USA.

29.   **ALEXANDER PATRICK CAMPBELL⁴ FLEMING** (Harwood Ontario Osborne³, Samuel², Daniel¹) was born on 13 Jun 1908 in Sandwich, Essex, Ontario, Canada. He died on 29 Jun 1983 in Encinitas, San Diego, California, USA. He married (1) **HELEN JEAN NICHOLSON** on 22 Mar 1930 in Santa Barbara, Santa Barbara, California, USA. She was born on 30 Apr 1909 in Santa Barbara, Santa Barbara, California, USA. He married (2) **CLARA LOIS HUNTER**, daughter of Lemna Joseph Hunter and Flora Hulda Knoll, on 05 Jul 1973 in San Diego, San Diego, California, USA. She was born on 29 Oct 1915 in Santa Cruz, Santa Cruz, California, USA. She died on 15 Jun 2006 in Cardiff-by-the-Sea, San Diego, California, USA.

Alexander Patrick Campbell Fleming and Clara Lois Hunter had the following child:

i.   LORNA ANN⁵ FLEMING was born on 14 Oct 1944 in Riverside, Riverside, California, USA. She died on 01 Mar 1974 in 1647 Garden, Vancouver, British Columbia, Canada (Homocide - severe blows to the head causing brain damage.). She married Edward Bruce Stanley on 24 Nov 1967 in San Diego, San Diego, California, USA. He was born on 14 Dec 1947 in San Diego, San Diego, California, USA.

30.   **AUDREY RUTH⁴ FLEMING** (Clarence Uriel Simcoe Bronte³, Samuel², Daniel¹) was born on 05 Aug 1901 in Detroit, Wayne, Michigan, USA. She died on 03 Feb 1975 in 622 E Lake Rd,

Hammondsport, Steuben, New York, USA. She married Guy Simmons Shoemaker, son of Floyd Monroe Shoemaker and Flora Lois Holmes, on 17 Apr 1923 in Pasadena, Los Angeles, California, USA. He was born on 04 Dec 1898 in Elmira, Chemung, New York, USA. He died on 09 Jul 1978 in Hammondsport, Steuben, New York, USA.

Guy Simmons Shoemaker and Audrey Ruth Fleming had the following children:

57.   i.   ARTHUR FLEMING[5] SHOEMAKER was born on 03 Sep 1924 in Elmira, Chemung, New York, USA. He died on 03 Jul 1992 in Elmira, Chemung, New York, USA. He married Mary Elizabeth Kinner, daughter of Jesse Lee Kinner MD and Margaret Emily Knapp, on 27 Dec 1945 in Elmira, Chemung, New York, USA. She was born on 16 Jul 1923 in Elmira, Chemung, New York, USA. She died on 21 Apr 2016 in Elmira, Chemung, New York, USA (Arnot Ogden Medical Centre).

58.   ii.   JOAN LOIS SHOEMAKER was born on 24 Oct 1926 in Elmira, Chemung, New York, USA. She died on 15 May 2005 in Rochester, Monroe, New York, USA. She married John Botsford Wilder, son of Hugo Traugott Wilder and Barbara Mary Botsford, on 18 Jun 1949 in Hammondsport, Steuben, New York, USA. He was born about 1927 in New Jersey, USA.

59.   iii.   AUDREY PATRICIA SHOEMAKER was born on 11 May 1928 in Elmira, Chemung, New York, USA. She died on 08 Mar 2001 in Mount Vernon, Skagit, Washington, USA. She married (1) DAVID BAIRD STORY, son of George Hall Story Jr and Milla Marcella Baird, on 18 Aug 1951 in Bath, Steuben, New York, USA. He was born on 31 Dec 1926 in Rochester, Monroe, New York, USA. He died on 11 Oct 2001 in Longview, Cowlitz, Washington, USA (Hospice Care Centre). She married (2) HOLLIS CHESTER WARNER on 04 Nov 1978 in King, Washington, USA. He was born on 13 Nov 1914 in Seattle, King, Washington, USA (Father: Chester Arthur Warner (1881-1960) / Mother: Maud Arlin Northey (1885-1960)). He died on 15 Dec 1980 in Belleview, King City, Washington, Oregon, USA.

31.   **VERA ALOHA[4] HOLMES** (Sarah Felicia Louisa Pell[3] Fleming, Samuel[2] Fleming, Daniel[1] Fleming) was born on 10 Aug 1889 in Toronto, Ontario, Canada. She died on 02 Sep 1975 in Toronto, Ontario, Canada. She married Archibald William Forbes DDS, son of William Forbes and Elizabeth Forbes, on 25 Dec 1912 in Old St. Andrew's Church, Toronto, Ontario, Canada. He was born on 01 Nov 1876 in Elma, Perth, Ontario, Canada. He died on 08 Mar 1942 in Toronto, Ontario, Canada (Cause o Death: Myocardistis - high blood pressure).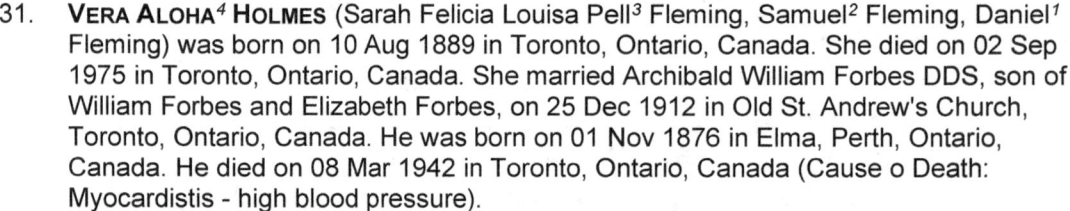

Archibald William Forbes DDS and Vera Aloha Holmes had the following children:

    i.   JEAN FLEMING[5] FORBES was born on 21 Dec 1914 in 13 Laburnam Av, Toronto, Ontario, Canada. She died on 17 Sep 1944 in Toronto, Ontario, Canada (Cause of Death: Coronary Thrombosis). She married Alfred Howard Moffat, son of Alfred Keith Moffat and Elizabeth Jane Roberts, on 11 Oct 1940 in Toronto, Ontario, Canada. He was born on 12 Jul 1912 in Toronto, Ontario, Canada. He died on 23 Mar 1991 in Palm Beach, Florida, USA.

60.   ii.   WILLIAM KEITH FORBES was born on 28 May 1917 in Toronto, Ontario, Canada. He died on 16 Jul 2001 in Mississauga, Niagara, Ontario, Canada. He married Eleanor Margaret Meyer, daughter of Albert John Meyer and Margaret Mary Jacobs, on 26 Sep 1946 in Toronto, Ontario, Canada. She was born on 08 Apr 1918 in Seattle, King, Washington, USA. She died on 01 Nov 2002 in Toronto, Ontario, Canada (St Joseph's Health Centre).

32.   **JOHN GUMSER[4] HOLMES** (Sarah Felicia Louisa Pell[3] Fleming, Samuel[2] Fleming, Daniel[1] Fleming) was born on 28 Sep 1890 in Toronto, Ontario, Canada. He died on 06 Jun 1953 in Toronto, Ontario, Canada. He married (1) **SARAH ETHEL CHATTERSON**. She was born on 10 Apr 1917 in Toronto, Ontario, Canada (Father: James Walter Chatterson (1890-1953) / Mother: Mary A Lees (1895-1963)). She died on 19 Dec 2003 in Shelburne, Dufferin, Ontario, Canada. He married (2) **IRENE MYRTLE DYNES MACKINTOSH**, daughter of John Argyll Macintosh and Rachel Ann Agnes Dynes Dewar Macintosh, in 1914. She was born on 05 Sep 1894 in Dufftown, Banffshire, Scotland. She died on 25 May 1993.

John Gumser Holmes had the following children:

61.   i.   HELEN ROSEMARY HOLMES was born on 13 Dec 1916 in Ontario, Canada. She died on 21 Nov 2013 in Toronto, Ontario, Canada (Cedarbrook Lodge). She married ARTHUR EDWARD CORBEAU. He was born on 18 Nov 1905 in Ontario, Canada (Father: Charles Edmund Corbeau (1881-1938) / Mother: Jane Doyle (1874-1948)). He died in 1981 in Toronto, Ontario, Canada.

        ii.   HOWARD RICHARD HOLMES was born on 05 Jun 1924 in Toronto, Ontario, Canada. He died on 10 Jun 1963 in Toronto, Ontario, Canada. He married Jean Taylor on 17 Jul 1958 in Toronto, Ontario, Canada. She was born on 27 Mar 1926 in Sheffield, Yorkshire, England. She died on 21 Nov 1991 in Scarborough, Toronto, Ontario, Canada.

John Gumser Holmes and Irene Myrtle Dynes Mackintosh had the following children:

61.   i.   HELEN ROSEMARY HOLMES was born on 13 Dec 1916 in Ontario, Canada. She died on 21 Nov 2013 in Toronto, Ontario, Canada (Cedarbrook Lodge). She married ARTHUR EDWARD CORBEAU. He was born on 18 Nov 1905 in Ontario, Canada (Father: Charles Edmund Corbeau (1881-1938) / Mother: Jane Doyle (1874-1948)). He died in 1981 in Toronto, Ontario, Canada.

        ii.   HOWARD RICHARD HOLMES was born on 05 Jun 1924 in Toronto, Ontario, Canada. He died on 10 Jun 1963 in Toronto, Ontario, Canada. He married Jean Taylor on 17 Jul 1958 in Toronto, Ontario, Canada. She was born on 27 Mar 1926 in Sheffield, Yorkshire, England. She died on 21 Nov 1991 in Scarborough, Toronto, Ontario, Canada.

33.   **THOMAS BYRON[4] HOLMES** (Sarah Felicia Louisa Pell[3] Fleming, Samuel[2] Fleming, Daniel[1] Fleming) was born on 10 Aug 1895 in York, Ontario, Canada. He died on 20 Aug 1979 in Toronto, Ontario, Canada (Cause of Death: Pneumionia). He married (1) **IRMA MARGARET MARTIN**, daughter of Edward Daniel Martin and Agnes Jane Perry, on 21 May 1924 in Winnipeg, Manitoba, Canada. She was born on 13 Sep 1896 in Manitoba, Canada. She died on 28 Nov 1989 in Toronto, Ontario, Canada. He married an unknown spouse on 21 May 1924 in Winnipeg, Manitoba, Canada.

Thomas Byron Holmes had the following children:

        i.   MARY[5] HOLMES was born on 16 Feb 1926 in Toronto, Ontario, Canada. She died on 20 Dec 2015 in Newmarket, York, Ontario, Canada. She married Anderson on 01 Nov 1947 in Toronto, Ontario, Canada. He was born about 1926 in (Likely), Toronto, Ontario, Canada.

        ii.   ANNE HOLMES was born on 28 Jul 1930 in Toronto, Ontario, Canada. She died on 12 Dec 2006 in Toronto, Ontario, Canada. She married STANLEY LANSDELL. He was born in Oct 1923. He died in 1987.

        iii.   THOMAS HARWOOD HOLMES was born on 17 Sep 1934 in Toronto, Ontario, Canada. He died on 22 Jun 2019. He married Margaret Elizabeth Merritt on 06 Jun 1962 in Toronto, Ontario, Canada. She was born on 18 Dec 1939 in Toronto, Ontario, Canada. She died on 17 Apr 2016.

Thomas Byron Holmes and Irma Margaret Martin had the following children:

        i.   MARY[5] HOLMES was born on 16 Feb 1926 in Toronto, Ontario, Canada. She died on 20 Dec 2015 in Newmarket, York, Ontario, Canada. She married Anderson on 01 Nov 1947 in Toronto, Ontario, Canada. He was born about 1926 in (Likely), Toronto, Ontario, Canada.

        ii.   ANNE HOLMES was born on 28 Jul 1930 in Toronto, Ontario, Canada. She died on 12 Dec 2006 in Toronto, Ontario, Canada. She married STANLEY LANSDELL. He was born in Oct 1923. He died in 1987.

        iii.   THOMAS HARWOOD HOLMES was born on 17 Sep 1934 in Toronto, Ontario, Canada. He died on 22 Jun 2019. He married Margaret Elizabeth Merritt on 06 Jun 1962 in Toronto, Ontario, Canada. She was born on 18 Dec 1939 in Toronto, Ontario, Canada. She died on 17 Apr 2016.

34. **OLGA EVELYN WENOWAE**[4] **HOLMES** (Sarah Felicia Louisa Pell[3] Fleming, Samuel[2] Fleming, Daniel[1] Fleming) was born on 10 May 1897 in Toronto, Ontario, Canada. She died on 02 Mar 1942 in (Likely), Toronto, Ontario, Canada. She married Russell McGill, son of William Robert McGill and Ann Eversfield, on 03 Sep 1918 in Halton, Ontario, Canada. He was born on 27 Mar 1894 in Toronto, Ontario, Canada. He died on 26 Feb 1927 in York, Ontario, Canada.

Russell McGill and Olga Evelyn Wenowae Holmes had the following child:

    i.   MARGARET[5] MCGILL was born about 1920 in Ontario, Canada.

35. **HERALD RICHARD**[4] **HOLMES** (Sarah Felicia Louisa Pell[3] Fleming, Samuel[2] Fleming, Daniel[1] Fleming) was born on 12 Oct 1905 in Huron, Ontario, Canada. He died on 03 Oct 1974 in Guelph, Wellington, Ontario, Canada. He married (1) **EHRMA I DEGUERRE** on 24 Aug 1935 in Buffalo, Erie, New York, USA. She was born on 23 Apr 1908 in Toronto, Ontario, Canada. She died in 1989.

Herald Richard Holmes had the following children:

    i.   WENDY[5] HOLMES was born about 1930 in (Likely), Toronto, Ontario, Canada.

    ii.   JOHN HOLMES was born about 1930 in (Likely), Toronto, Ontario, Canada.

Herald Richard Holmes and Ehrma I DeGuerre had the following children:

    i.   WENDY[5] HOLMES was born about 1930 in (Likely), Toronto, Ontario, Canada.

    ii.   JOHN HOLMES was born about 1930 in (Likely), Toronto, Ontario, Canada.

36. **WILLIAM EVERETTE**[4] **SCOTTEN JR** (Florence Selenica Viola[3] Fleming, Samuel[2] Fleming, Daniel[1] Fleming) was born on 24 Aug 1904 in Detroit, Wayne, Michigan, USA. He died on 27 Nov 1958 in Orange, California, USA. He married Caroline Cornelia Tarcea, daughter of Dumitru Dan Tarcea and Maria Fritea, on 01 May 1943 in District of Columbia, USA. She was born on 21 Jun 1917 in Akron, Summit, Ohio, USA. She died on 02 Apr 2003 in La Habra, Orange, California, USA.

William Everette Scotten Jr and Caroline Cornelia Tarcea had the following child:

    i.   WILLIAM E[5] SCOTTEN was born on 20 Jan 1944 in (Likely), Cook, Illinois, USA. He married Kay Mason on 10 Dec 1966 in Woodbridge, Prince William, Virginia, USA. She was born on 04 Jul 1943 in Henry, Franklin, Virginia, USA.

37. **JOSEPH LACY**[4] **MARTIN** (Jasper F[3], Mary Ann[2] Fleming, Daniel[1] Fleming) was born on 02 May 1880 in Ypsilanti, Washtenaw, Michigan, USA. He died on 13 Feb 1968 in Ventura, California, USA. He married (1) **ALMA EMMA ANDERSON**, daughter of Marinus Andersen and Susan Nielson, on 01 Dec 1937 in Fort Dodge, Webster, Iowa, USA. She was born on 27 Jun 1909 in Palmer, Merrick, Nebraska, USA. She died on 08 Mar 1998 in Tempe, Maricopa, Arizona, USA. He married (2) **HARRIET JANE COOK**, daughter of Charles Henry Cook and Sabra Ann Russell, on 21 Jun 1909 in Le Mars, Plymouth, Iowa, USA. She was born about 1888 in Vermillion, Clay, South Dakota, USA. She died on 11 Jan 1976 in Escondido, San Diego, California, USA.

Joseph Lacy Martin and Alma Emma Anderson had the following children:

    i.   CHARLES EDWIN[5] MARTIN was born on 30 Jan 1938 in Sioux City, Woodbury, Iowa, USA.

62.   ii.   RICHARD JAMES MARTIN was born on 04 May 1939 in Sioux City, Woodbury, Iowa, USA. He died on 31 Oct 2011 in Berea, Madison, Kentucky, USA. He married JUDITH FAYE STEWART. She was born about 1945 in (Likely), Kentucky, USA. She died on 01 Jan 2017 in Berea, Madison, Kentucky, USA (She started a nonprofit to empower rural Appalachian communities.).

Joseph Lacy Martin and Harriet Jane Cook had the following children:

63.   iii.   JOSEPH VARDEMAN MARTIN was born on 12 Nov 1911 in Vermillion, Clay, South Dakota, USA. He died on 02 Apr 1997 in Lexington, Fayette, Kentucky, USA. He married (1) JANE SOPHIE GROVER, daughter of Clarence Wesley Grover and Sophia Pauline Hawlish, on 15 Feb 1941 in Northwood, Worth, Iowa, USA. She was born on 31 Jan 1918 in Minneapolis, Hennepin, Minnesota, USA. She died on 30 May 1979 in Lexington, Fayette, Kentucky,

USA. He married (2) SHIRLEY ANN WAMSLEY on 06 Nov 1937 in Minneapolis, Hennepin, Minnesota, USA. She was born about 1916. She died on 05 Feb 1996 in Waukesha, Wisconsin, USA. He married (3) LILLIAN FRANCES HOLLAND, daughter of William R Holland Jr and Lucretia U Lively, on 18 May 1985 in Fayette, Kentucky, USA. She was born on 07 Oct 1917 in Adams, Decatur, Indiana, USA (Father: William Russell "Willie" Holland (1895-1958) / Mother: Lucretia Uletha Lively (1897-1990)). She died on 16 Aug 2003.

iv. ELAINE MARTIN was born on 13 Mar 1914 in Vermillion, Clay, South Dakota, USA. She died on 05 Oct 2010 in Ventura, California, USA. She married (1) ROBERT DALE BUCK, son of William Harrison Buck and Marie Helena Dale, in 1939 in Sioux Falls, Minnehaha, South Dakota, USA. He was born on 23 Jul 1914 in Madison, Lake, South Dakota, USA. He died on 28 Feb 1979 in San Diego, California, USA.

38. **ELIZABETH PERRY[4] MARTIN** (Edward Daniel[3], Mary Ann[2] Fleming, Daniel[1] Fleming) was born on 14 Jul 1882 in Carleton, Ontario, Canada. She died in 1962 in Toronto, Ontario, Canada. She married Albert Courtney Gillespie, son of George Edward Gillespie and Mary Meudell, in 1903. He was born on 10 Nov 1877 in Toronto, Ontario, Canada. He died on 09 May 1943 in Toronto, Ontario, Canada.

Albert Courtney Gillespie and Elizabeth Perry Martin had the following children:

i. EDWARD MARTIN[5] GILLESPIE was born on 28 Aug 1904 in Toronto, Ontario, Canada. He died in 1965 in Toronto, Ontario, Canada. He married Florence Jean Hyland, daughter of Frederick Gordon Hyland and Florence Augusta Peters, on 06 Nov 1937 in Toronto, Ontario, Canada. She was born on 19 Oct 1915 in Toronto, Ontario, Canada. She died on 04 Apr 1969.

64. ii. ELIZABETH BROCK GILLESPIE was born in 1906 in Toronto, Ontario, Canada. She married (1) CLIFFORD SIFTON in 1962. He was born in 1893. He died in 1976 in Toronto, Ontario, Canada. She married (2) FRANCIS HERBERT CRISPO, son of Frank William Sidney Crispo and Mary Louise Gertrude Tiffany, on 10 Oct 1931 in Toronto, Ontario, Canada. He was born on 02 Oct 1899 in Toronto, Ontario, Canada. He died in 1960.

iii. DORIS M GILLESPIE was born on 23 Jul 1915 in Toronto, Ontario, Canada. She died on 02 Mar 2004 in Toronto, Ontario, Canada.

39. **JEAN AGNES[4] MARTIN** (Edward Daniel[3], Mary Ann[2] Fleming, Daniel[1] Fleming) was born on 22 Jul 1886 in Carleton, Ontario, Canada. She died on 14 Dec 1957 in Ontario, Canada. She married Daniel Campbell MacLachlan, son of Alexander Campbell MacLachlan and Jane Garson, on 08 Oct 1912 in Winnipeg, Manitoba, Canada. He was born on 15 Oct 1882 in Guelph, Wellington, Ontario, Canada. He died on 27 Apr 1964 in Toronto, Ontario, Canada.

Daniel Campbell MacLachlan and Jean Agnes Martin had the following children:

i. GRAHAM MARTIN[5] MACLACHLAN was born in 1914 in Winnipeg, Manitoba, Canada. He died in 1982 in Toronto, Ontario, Canada. He married MARY HOWARD MALIWRAITH. She was born in 1915 in Toronto, Ontario, Canada.

65. ii. CAMPBELL MARTIN MACLACHLAN was born on 24 Jan 1917 in Winnipeg, Manitoba, Canada. He died on 06 Mar 1997 in Beaverton, Durham, Ontario, Canada. He married Mary Patricia Louise Oxley, daughter of Duncan M Oxley and Patricia Robt Boyd, about 1946 in (Likely), Toronto, Ontario, Canada. She was born on 21 Jan 1915 in Toronto, Ontario, Canada. She died on 14 Jan 1983 in Ontario, Canada.

iii. JOHN MARTIN MACLACHLAN was born on 20 Aug 1918 in Winnipeg, Manitoba, Canada. He died on 05 Feb 1919 in Winnipeg, Manitoba, Canada.

iv. EDWARD MARTIN MACLACHLAN was born on 20 Aug 1919 in Winnipeg, Manitoba, Canada. He died on 15 Jul 1943 in Sicilia, Italy (Cause of Death: Killed In Action).

66. v. DAVID ALEXANDER MACLACHLAN was born on 28 Oct 1925 in Winnipeg, Manitoba, Canada. He died in 2000 in Oakville, Halton, Ontario, Canada. He married Margaret Jean Gunn on 09 Jan 1953 in Vancouver, British Columbia, Canada. She was born on 09 May 1928 in Vancouver, British Columbia, Canada.

40. **MARY FLEMING⁴ MARTIN** (Edward Daniel³, Mary Ann² Fleming, Daniel¹ Fleming) was born on 21 May 1894 in Winnipeg, Manitoba, Canada. She died on 12 May 1991 in Vancouver, British Columbia, Canada. She married Kenneth Gordon Nairn, son of John Nairn Jr and Amy Gertrude Rides, on 16 Dec 1920 in Winnipeg, Manitoba, Canada. He was born on 09 Nov 1898 in Edinburgh Newington, Midlothian, Scotland. He died on 29 Oct 1988 in Vancouver, British Columbia, Canada (Death year cited in wife's obituary.).

Kenneth Gordon Nairn and Mary Fleming Martin had the following children:

67.   i.   KENNETH ROGER⁵ NAIRN was born about 1923 in Rockcliffe Park, Vancouver, British Columbia, Canada. He died on 10 Jun 2006 in Vancouver, British Columbia, Canada. He married Sarah Elizabeth Gwendoline Wallace, daughter of James F A Wallace, on 08 Dec 1945 in Rockcliffe Park, Ottawa, Ontario, Canada. She was born about 1923 in (Likely), Vancouver, British Columbia, Canada. She died after 2006.

        ii.   MARCUS O NAIRN was born about 1926 in Vancouver, British Columbia, Canada. He died after 2006.

       iii.   JANE NAIRN was born about 1929 in Vancouver, British Columbia, Canada.

41. **IRMA MARGARET⁴ MARTIN** (Edward Daniel³, Mary Ann² Fleming, Daniel¹ Fleming) was born on 13 Sep 1896 in Manitoba, Canada. She died on 28 Nov 1989 in Toronto, Ontario, Canada. She married (2) **THOMAS BYRON HOLMES**, son of Richard Huron Holmes and Sarah Felicia Louisa Pell Fleming, on 21 May 1924 in Winnipeg, Manitoba, Canada. He was born on 10 Aug 1895 in York, Ontario, Canada. He died on 20 Aug 1979 in Toronto, Ontario, Canada (Cause of Death: Pneumionia).

Irma Margaret Martin had the following children:

        i.   MARY⁵ HOLMES was born on 16 Feb 1926 in Toronto, Ontario, Canada. She died on 20 Dec 2015 in Newmarket, York, Ontario, Canada. She married Anderson on 01 Nov 1947 in Toronto, Ontario, Canada. He was born about 1926 in (Likely), Toronto, Ontario, Canada.

        ii.   ANNE HOLMES was born on 28 Jul 1930 in Toronto, Ontario, Canada. She died on 12 Dec 2006 in Toronto, Ontario, Canada. She married STANLEY LANSDELL. He was born in Oct 1923. He died in 1987.

       iii.   THOMAS HARWOOD HOLMES was born on 17 Sep 1934 in Toronto, Ontario, Canada. He died on 22 Jun 2019. He married Margaret Elizabeth Merritt on 06 Jun 1962 in Toronto, Ontario, Canada. She was born on 18 Dec 1939 in Toronto, Ontario, Canada. She died on 17 Apr 2016.

Thomas Byron Holmes and Irma Margaret Martin had the following children:

        i.   MARY⁵ HOLMES was born on 16 Feb 1926 in Toronto, Ontario, Canada. She died on 20 Dec 2015 in Newmarket, York, Ontario, Canada. She married Anderson on 01 Nov 1947 in Toronto, Ontario, Canada. He was born about 1926 in (Likely), Toronto, Ontario, Canada.

        ii.   ANNE HOLMES was born on 28 Jul 1930 in Toronto, Ontario, Canada. She died on 12 Dec 2006 in Toronto, Ontario, Canada. She married STANLEY LANSDELL. He was born in Oct 1923. He died in 1987.

       iii.   THOMAS HARWOOD HOLMES was born on 17 Sep 1934 in Toronto, Ontario, Canada. He died on 22 Jun 2019. He married Margaret Elizabeth Merritt on 06 Jun 1962 in Toronto, Ontario, Canada. She was born on 18 Dec 1939 in Toronto, Ontario, Canada. She died on 17 Apr 2016.

42. **ANNA JOYCE⁴ WHITE** (Anna Davenport³ Keeler, Lucy A² Fleming, Daniel¹ Fleming) was born on 30 Jul 1902 in Wakefield, Clay, Kansas, USA. She died on 30 Jan 1992 in Phoenix, Maricopa, Arizona, USA. She married Harvey Cyrus Osborne LLD, son of Fred Osborne and Emma Louise Paul, on 20 Oct 1929 in 1207 East Franklin Apt E, Lawrence, Douglas, Kansas, USA. He was born on 07 Oct 1898 in Ashland, Clark, Kansas, USA. He died on 21 Oct 1967 in Globe, Gila, Arizona, USA.

Harvey Cyrus Osborne LLD and Anna Joyce White had the following children:

68.   i.   JOYCE ANN⁵ OSBORNE was born on 26 Jul 1933 in Wichita, Sedgwick, Kansas, USA. She died about Sep 2017 in Gila, Arizona, USA. She married Melvin Monroe Montgomery, son of James Monroe Montgomery and Ula May Hobbs, on 31 Jan 1953 in Peridot, Gila, Arizona, USA (met her husband Melvin Montgomery at the Justa Café in Globe.). He was born on 03 Aug 1931 in Oklahoma, USA. He died on 06 Sep 2015 in Mesa, Maricopa, Arizona, USA.

     ii.   SUZANNE OSBORNE was born on 07 Mar 1942. She married (1) ROBERT E HALLIDAY between 1968-1985. He was born about 1943 in (Likely), Arizona, USA. She married (2) JOHN L WEBB, son of Cecil H Webb and Mona Evans, on 20 Aug 1962 in San Diego, California, USA. He was born on 14 Mar 1943 in St Joseph, Buchanan, Missouri, USA. He died on 29 May 2008 in Nashville, Nash, North Carolina, USA.

     iii.   PAUL STEPHEN OSBORNE was born about 1945 in (Likely), Kansas, USA. He married Dorothy Jean Moulton, daughter of Albert Moulton, on 18 Apr 1971 in Wellsville, Allegany, New York, USA. She was born on 04 Aug 1945 in Washington, District of Columbia, USA. She died on 26 Dec 1994.

43.   **LEWIS BURTON⁴ WHITE** (Anna Davenport³ Keeler, Lucy A² Fleming, Daniel¹ Fleming) was born on 12 May 1906 in Wakefield, Clay, Kansas, USA (Father: Burton White / Mother: Ann D). He died in Jul 1982 in Topeka, Shawnee, Kansas, USA (Cause of Death: Heart Attack). He married Marion Adelle Fletcher, daughter of Burton Raymond Fletcher and Elsie Victoria Boutwell, on 05 Apr 1930 in Lawrence, Douglas, Kansas, USA. She was born on 15 Jan 1913 in Nebraska, USA. She died on 14 Feb 1983 in Topeka, Shawnee, Kansas, USA (Topeka Hospital).

Lewis Burton White and Marion Adelle Fletcher had the following children:

69.   i.   MARILEW⁵ WHITE was born on 06 Jan 1932 in Nebraska, USA. She died on 17 May 2011 in Yadkinville, Yadkin, North Carolina, USA. She married (1) BERNARD LEROY VAUGHN, son of Timothy Bernard Vaughn and Lydia Belle Viles, about 1958 (2nd marriage). He was born on 01 Aug 1928 in Topeka, Shawnee, Kansas, USA. He died on 18 Nov 2012 in Topeka, Shawnee, Kansas, USA. She married (2) ROY J SCHELLER on 19 Dec 1949 in Topeka, Shawnee, Kansas, USA (1st marriage). He was born on 16 Aug 1926 in Racine, Racine, Wisconsin, USA. She married (3) EUGENE H BLOCKER on 23 Nov 1967 (3rd marriage). He was born on 15 Mar 1936 in Georgia, USA. She married (4) WILLIAM HEMRICK. He was born about 1932.

70.   ii.   JAMES LEWIS WHITE was born about 1936 in Topeka, Shawnee, Kansas, USA. He died on 23 Jan 2018 in Junction City, Geary, Kansas, USA. He married Ruby Fay Millard, daughter of Reuben West Millard and Belva A Roth, on 02 Jul 1959 (Introduced together by sister Mary Lou Hemrick.). She was born on 14 Mar 1931 in Geneseo, Rice, Kansas, USA (Father: Reuben W. Millard (1891-) / Mother: Belva A. Roth (1903-)). She died on 13 Aug 2018 in Bentley, Sedgwick, Kansas, USA.

71.   iii.   THOMAS BURT WHITE was born on 06 Feb 1945 in Topeka, Shawnee, Kansas, USA. He died on 19 Aug 2013 in Tecumseh, Shawnee, Kansas, USA. He married (1) JANICE ALICE JESSOP. She was born on 07 Jul 1947 in Topeka, Shawnee, Kansas, USA (Father: Wayne Winfred Jessop (1907-1967) / Mother: Beryl Beatrice Disney (1911-2004)). She died on 06 Feb 2013 in Topeka, Shawnee, Kansas, USA. He married (2) SANDRA SUSAN BIGHAM about 1968. She was born on 30 Aug 1941 in Brownsville, Cameron, Texas, USA (Father: Howard Raymond Bigham (1906-1977) / Mother: Iona Mae "Tony" Brown (1912-1993)). She died on 16 Mar 2010 in Marysville, Snohomish, Washington, USA. He married (3) LILA MAY BRITTAIN DEJARNETTE on 21 Aug 1976 in Elko, Elko, Nevada, USA. She was born about 1945 in (Likely), Kansas, USA.

44. **MARJORIE[5] LLOYD-SMITH** (Marjorie[4] Fleming, Arthur Samuel Henry[3] Fleming, Samuel[2] Fleming, Daniel[1] Fleming) was born on 18 Jul 1918 in New York, New York, USA. She died on 30 Mar 2004 in Washington, District of Columbia, USA. She married (1) **GEORGE MARSHALL HORNBLOWER**, son of George Sanford Hornblower and Dorothy Marshall, on 10 Nov 1940 in Elmira, Chemung, New York, USA. He was born on 19 Nov 1917 in New York, New York, USA (Father: George Sanford Hornblower (1884-) / Mother: Dorothy Marshall (1886-1968)). He died on 06 Oct 2006 in Washington, District of Columbia, USA.

George Marshall Hornblower and Marjorie Lloyd-Smith had the following children:

    i.   MARJORIE[6] HORNBLOWER was born on 14 Feb 1942 in New York, New York, USA. She married JOHNSON. He was born about 1945 in (Likely), Washington, District of Columbia, USA.

72.   ii.   JONATHAN MARSH HORNBLOWER was born about 1943 in (Likely), Washington, District of Columbia, USA. He married Alexandra Cheston Tower, daughter of Whitney Tower and Frances Cheston, on 29 May 1971 in Bedford, Westchester, New York, USA. She was born on 21 Apr 1949 in Ohio, USA.

    iii.   JENNY HORNBLOWER was born about 1945 in (Likely), Washington, District of Columbia, USA. She married LAWRENCE. He was born about 1945 in (Likely), Washington, District of Columbia, USA.

    iv.   NANCY ROSILLA HORNBLOWER was born on 11 Jan 1946 in Washington, District of Columbia, USA. She died on 07 Apr 2007 in San Diego, California, USA. She married (1) GEORGE MARTIN RICE on 12 Jun 1982 in Los Angeles, California, USA. He was born about 1945 in (Likely), California, USA. She married (2) JOHN FREDERICK COSGROVE about 1967. He was born on 13 Jul 1944 in Los Angeles, California, USA.

45. **HAROLD FLEMING[5] KERRIGAN** (Frances Maud[4] Fleming, Oscar Ernest[3] Fleming LLD, Samuel[2] Fleming, Daniel[1] Fleming) was born on 10 Jun 1917 in Sandwich, Essex, Ontario, Canada. He died on 03 Sep 1993 in Knowlton, Brome-Missisquoi, Quebec, Canada. He married (1) **VIRGINIA ERNESTINE PORTER**, daughter of Ernest Albee Porter and Emma Bernice Porter, on 12 Aug 1944 in Brookline, Norfolk, Massachusetts, USA. She was born in 1922 in Brookline, Norfolk, Massachusetts, USA. He married an unknown spouse in 1944 in Brookline, Norfolk, Massachusetts, USA.

Harold Fleming Kerrigan and Virginia Ernestine Porter had the following children:

    i.   STEPHEN[6] KERRIGAN was born about 1945 in (Likely), Brookline, Norfolk, Massachusetts, USA.

    ii.   MEREDITH LYNN KERRIGAN was born about 1945 in (Likely), Brookline, Norfolk, Massachusetts, USA. She married Clement Daniel McCarthy on 12 Oct 1963 in Alameda, California, USA. He was born on 25 Jan 1933 in San Francisco, California, USA.

73.   iii.   GEOFFREY BLAIR KERRIGAN was born about 1946 in (Likely), Toronto, Ontario, Canada. He died on 12 Oct 2020 in Georgian Bay, Ontario, Canada (Cause of Death: Cancer). He married Heather () in 1968.

46. **PETER FREDERICK[5] KERRIGAN** (Frances Maud[4] Fleming, Oscar Ernest[3] Fleming LLD, Samuel[2] Fleming, Daniel[1] Fleming) was born on 24 Mar 1919 in Walkerville, Essex, Ontario, Canada. He died on 01 Jun 1992 in Knowlton, Brome-Missisquoi, Quebec, Canada. He married Margaret Claire Fisher, daughter of Philip Sydney Fisher and Margaret Southam, on 15 May 1946 in Montréal, Montréal (Urban Agglomeration), Quebec, Canada. She was born about 1924 in (Likely), Montréal, Montréal (Urban Agglomeration), Quebec, Canada.

Peter Frederick Kerrigan and Margaret Claire Fisher had the following children:

    i.   CYNTHIA FRANCES[6] KERRIGAN was born on 29 May 1947 in Westmount, Montréal, Montréal (Urban Agglomeration), Quebec, Canada. She died on 17 Apr 1952 in Westmount, Montréal, Montréal (Urban Agglomeration), Quebec, Canada.

74.   ii.   CAROLYN KERRIGAN MD was born about 1950 in (Likely), Westmount, Montréal (Urban Agglomeration), Quebec, Canada. She married (1) LINTON. He was born about 1950 in (Likely), Montréal, Montréal (Urban Agglomeration), Quebec, Canada. She married (2) WARREN YOUNG SOPER III, son of Warren Young Soper II and P Claude Duval, on 18 Aug 1973 in Knowlton, Brome-Missisquoi, Quebec, Canada (in home of bride's parents). He was born about 1950 in (Likely), Montréal, Montréal (Urban Agglomeration), Quebec, Canada.

       iii.   LUCY KERRIGAN was born about 1950 in (Likely), Westmount, Montréal (Urban Agglomeration), Quebec, Canada.

       iv.   CHRISTOPHER KERRIGAN was born about 1950 in (Likely), Westmount, Montréal (Urban Agglomeration), Quebec, Canada.

       v.   PAMELA CLAIRE KERRIGAN was born on 05 Nov 1952 in Westmount, Montréal, Montréal (Urban Agglomeration), Quebec, Canada. She died on 27 Dec 1952 in Westmount, Montréal, Montréal (Urban Agglomeration), Quebec, Canada.

       vi.   PHILIP S KERRIGAN was born about 1955 in (Likely), Westmount, Montréal (Urban Agglomeration), Quebec, Canada.

47.   **BARBARA FRANCES[5] KERRIGAN** (Frances Maud[4] Fleming, Oscar Ernest[3] Fleming LLD, Samuel[2] Fleming, Daniel[1] Fleming) was born on 04 Jul 1920 in Walkerville, Essex, Ontario, Canada. She died on 21 May 2007 in Ottawa, Ontario, Canada. She married William Donald Munro Sr, son of William Munro and Ethel Hall, on 06 Jul 1953 in Montréal, Montréal (Urban Agglomeration), Quebec, Canada. He was born on 29 Mar 1922 in Titusville, Crawford, Pennsylvania, USA. He died on 28 Feb 2007 in Ottawa, Ontario, Canada.

William Donald Munro Sr and Barbara Frances Kerrigan had the following child:

       i.   ALISON ANN[6] MUNRO was born on 05 Nov 1963 in Ottawa, Ottawa, Ontario, Canada. She died on 14 Nov 1963 in Ottawa, Ontario, Canada.

48.   **GEOFFREY MOORE[5] KERRIGAN** (Frances Maud[4] Fleming, Oscar Ernest[3] Fleming LLD, Samuel[2] Fleming, Daniel[1] Fleming) was born on 06 Nov 1921 in London, Middlesex, Ontario, Canada. He died on 21 Feb 2013 in Middlesex Hospice, Middlesex, Connecticut, USA. He married Marjorie Brooks, daughter of Harry Brooks and Mary Hannah Lavender, on 25 Mar 1943 in Cleveland, Yorkshire, England. She was born on 12 Sep 1921 in Ormesby, Yorkshire, England. She died on 13 May 2009 in Essex, Middlesex, Connecticut, USA.

Geoffrey Moore Kerrigan and Marjorie Brooks had the following children:

       i.   DAVID[6] KERRIGAN was born about 1945 in (Likely), Eston, Middlesbrough, Connecticut, USA. He married Jean Lamont, daughter of E S Lamont, on 07 Jun 1969. She was born about 1950.

       ii.   MICHAEL KERRIGAN was born about 1947 in (Likely), Eston, Middlesbrough, Connecticut, USA. He married (1) KIMBERLY M WARNER on 18 Aug 2001 in Washoe, Nevada, USA. She was born about 1950. He married (2) JANE A ATHAN on 23 Aug 1970 in Stamford, Fairfield, Connecticut, USA. She was born about 1948.

       iii.   BRIAN PETER KERRIGAN was born about 1950 in Eston, Middlesbrough, Connecticut, USA.

49.   **JOCELYN ANN[5] KERRIGAN** (Frances Maud[4] Fleming, Oscar Ernest[3] Fleming LLD, Samuel[2] Fleming, Daniel[1] Fleming) was born on 25 Sep 1926 in Goderich, Huron, Ontario, Canada. She died on 11 Feb 1995 in Ottawa, Ontario, Canada (Cause of Death: cancer). She married Robin Benitz on 02 May 1959 in Montréal, Montréal (Urban Agglomeration), Quebec, Canada (Personal notes --> https://www.ancestry.ca/family-tree/person/tree/111982665/person/370093036050/facts). He was born about 1925.

Robin Benitz and Jocelyn Ann Kerrigan had the following children:

       i.   NANCY[6] BENITZ was born about 1950. She married SMALE. He was born about 1950.

75.   ii.   VANESSA BENITZ was born about 1950. She married GUY LAFRAMBOISE. He was

born about 1950.

    iii.   NICHOLAS BENITZ was born about 1950.

50.   **JEAN ELIZABETH**⁵ **FLEMING** (Kenneth Eldon⁴, Oscar Ernest³ LLD, Samuel², Daniel¹) was born on 02 Mar 1927 in Montréal, Montréal (Urban Agglomeration), Quebec, Canada. She died on 24 Nov 2008 in Greenwich, Fairfield, Connecticut, USA. She married (1) **SYDNEY ANGLIN WOODD-CAHUSAC REV**, son of Kenneth Anglin Woodd-Cahusac and Beatrice Maude Barry, on 01 Dec 1951 in Niagara St, Riverside, Missaukee, Michigan, USA. He was born on 02 Apr 1918 in New York, New York, USA. He died on 03 Jan 2004 in Greenwich, Fairfield, Connecticut, USA.

Sydney Anglin Woodd-Cahusac Rev and Jean Elizabeth Fleming had the following children:

76.   i.   ANN BLYTHE⁶ WOODD-CAHUSAC was born about 1954. She married Matthew J Neary Jr, son of Matthew J Neary and Cynthia Audrey Evelyn, on 28 Oct 1995 in Greenwich, Fairfield, Connecticut, USA. He was born on 10 Apr 1954 in New York, New York, USA.

77.   ii.   LEE WOODD-CAHUSAC was born about 1955 in Greenwich, Fairfield, Connecticut, USA (Per facebook). She married COWANS. He was born about 1955.

    iii.   KENNETH WOODD-CAHUSAC was born on 08 Jul 1956 in New York, New York, USA. He died on 11 Mar 2017 in Riverside, Fairfield, Connecticut, USA.

51.   **CATHERINE ANN GORDON**⁵ **CLEATHER** (Caroline Beatrice⁴ Fleming, Oscar Ernest³ Fleming LLD, Samuel² Fleming, Daniel¹ Fleming) was born on 21 Jun 1928 in (Likely), New York, New York, USA. She died on 27 Mar 2017 in North York General Hospital, Toronto, Ontario, Canada. She married Joseph Louis Charles Vanderheyden on 14 Apr 1956 in Church of the Lady of the Assumption, Toronto, Ontario, Canada. He was born about 1928. He died in 2001 in Toronto, Ontario, Canada.

Joseph Louis Charles "Duke Vanderheyden" Vanderheyden and Catherine Ann Gordon Cleather had the following children:

    i.   MICHAEL⁶ VANDERHEYDEN was born in 1960 in Toronto, Ontario, Canada. He died in 2007.

    ii.   CAROLYN VANDERHEYDEN was born about 28 Oct 1962 in Toronto, Ontario, Canada. She married DENZIL FAIRE. He was born about 1962 in Ottawa, Ontario, Canada.

52.   **EDWARD GORDON**⁵ **CLEATHER** (Caroline Beatrice⁴ Fleming, Oscar Ernest³ Fleming LLD, Samuel² Fleming, Daniel¹ Fleming) was born on 11 Dec 1929 in St John, Saint John, New Brunswick, Canada. He died on 06 Aug 2021 in Toronto, Ontario, Canada. He married Joan Margaret Allen, daughter of W Graham Allen, on 28 Nov 1959 in Halifax, Nova Scotia, Canada. She was born about 1930 in (Likely), Windsor, Essex, Ontario, Canada. She died after 2021.

Edward Gordon Cleather and Joan Margaret Allen had the following children:

    i.   GRAHAM⁶ CLEATHER was born about 1965 in (Likely), Montréal, Montréal (Urban Agglomeration), Quebec, Canada.

78.   ii.   CAROLYN GORDON CLEATHER was born in Feb 1965 in Montréal, Montréal (Urban Agglomeration), Quebec, Canada. She married RICHARD KIEL BROOK. He was born in Aug 1959 in Beaconsfield, Montréal (Urban Agglomeration), Quebec, Canada.

53.   **GILLIAN GORDON**⁵ **CLEATHER** (Caroline Beatrice⁴ Fleming, Oscar Ernest³ Fleming LLD, Samuel² Fleming, Daniel¹ Fleming) was born in Jul 1937 (Kensington, London, England). She married (1) **YOUNG**. He was born about 1950. She married (2) **HAROLD PAUL CUSHING HAYNES**. He was born in 1937.

Harold Paul Cushing Haynes and Gillian Gordon Cleather had the following children:

    i.   BRYAN⁶ HAYNES was born about 1955 in (Likely), Kitchener, Waterloo, Ontario, Canada.

    ii.   KATHERINE HAYNES was born about 1960 in (Likely), Kitchener, Waterloo, Ontario, Canada.

       iii.   SUSAN HAYNES was born about 1960 in (Likely), Kitchener, Waterloo, Ontario, Canada.

       iv.   KEVIN HAYNES was born about 1961 in (Likely), Kitchener, Waterloo, Ontario, Canada. He died on 12 Jul 1995 in Squamish, British Columbia, Canada.

54.   **DAVID FLEMING**[5] **WRIGHT** (Bertha Ernesta[4] Fleming, Oscar Ernest[3] Fleming LLD, Samuel[2] Fleming, Daniel[1] Fleming) was born about 1934 in (Likely), 10 Bridgetown Rd, Toronto, Ontario, Canada. He married Mary Ann Langmuir, daughter of Bryant Langmuir, on 09 Nov 1960 in Lewiston, Niagara, New York, USA. She was born about 1935.

David Fleming Wright and Mary Ann Langmuir had the following children:

       i.   DAVID LANGMUIR[6] WRIGHT was born about 1964 in Toronto, Ontario, Canada. He married Marjorie () on 06 Aug 2006. She was born about 1980.

       ii.   SASHA WRIGHT was born about 1968 in (Likely), Toronto, Ontario, Canada. She married DARLING. He was born about 1968 in (Likely), Toronto, Ontario, Canada.

       iii.   ALEXANDRA WRIGHT was born about 10 Jan 1975 in (Likely), Toronto, Ontario, Canada. She married ELLING. He was born about 1975 in (Likely), Toronto, Ontario, Canada.

55.   **CHARLES FLEMING**[5] **GROSS** (Jean Helene[4] Fleming, Oscar Ernest[3] Fleming LLD, Samuel[2] Fleming, Daniel[1] Fleming) was born on 22 Mar 1930 in Toronto, Ontario, Canada. He died on 11 Aug 2021 in Montréal, Montréal (Urban Agglomeration), Quebec, Canada. He married Rosamond Aletha Jones, daughter of Arthur Frederick Hill Jones and Aletha Rosamond Chestnut, on 13 Feb 1954 in Oakville, Halton, Ontario, Canada. She was born on 17 Feb 1931 in Toronto, Ontario, Canada. She died on 07 Nov 2017 in Ottawa, Ontario, Canada.

Charles Fleming Gross and Rosamond Aletha Jones had the following children:

       i.   KEVIN CHARLES[6] GROSS was born on 22 Dec 1955 in (Likely), Toronto, Ontario, Canada. He married Carol Ann Hlad, daughter of Harold Dalton Hlad and Shirley Jean Glas, on 01 Jul 1977 in Wyckoff, Bergen, New Jersey, USA. She was born about 1960 in (Likely), Scranton, Lackawanna, Pennsylvania, USA.

79.   ii.   ANDREW ARTHUR GROSS was born about 1960 in (Likely), Toronto, Ontario, Canada. He married NORA (). She was born about 1960 in (Likely), Montréal, Montréal (Urban Agglomeration), Quebec, Canada.

       iii.   DAVID WHITNEY GROSS was born on 28 Jul 1960 in Canton, Stark, Ohio, USA. He married Renae L Reed on 24 Aug 1997 in Stark, Ohio, USA. She was born about 1961.

56.   **PHILIP NORCROSS**[5] **GROSS JR** (Jean Helene[4] Fleming, Oscar Ernest[3] Fleming LLD, Samuel[2] Fleming, Daniel[1] Fleming) was born about 1940 in (Likely), Montréal, Montréal (Urban Agglomeration), Quebec, Canada. He married Norma Jean Beattie, daughter of Norman Karl Beattie, on 29 Jun 1964 in Fredericton, York, New Brunswick, Canada. She was born in 1941 in (Likely), Montréal, Montréal (Urban Agglomeration), Quebec, Canada.

Philip Norcross Gross Jr and Norma Jean Beattie had the following child:

       i.   DAVID[6] NORCROSS was born about 1960 in Ottawa, Ontario, Canada.

57.   **ARTHUR FLEMING**[5] **SHOEMAKER** (Audrey Ruth[4] Fleming, Clarence Uriel Simcoe Bronte[3] Fleming, Samuel[2] Fleming, Daniel[1] Fleming) was born on 03 Sep 1924 in Elmira, Chemung, New York, USA. He died on 03 Jul 1992 in Elmira, Chemung, New York, USA. He married Mary Elizabeth Kinner, daughter of Jesse Lee Kinner MD and Margaret Emily Knapp, on 27 Dec 1945 in Elmira, Chemung, New York, USA. She was born on 16 Jul 1923 in Elmira, Chemung, New York, USA. She died on 21 Apr 2016 in Elmira, Chemung, New York, USA (Arnot Ogden Medical Centre).

Arthur Fleming Shoemaker and Mary Elizabeth Kinner had the following children:

i.   JANET[6] SHOEMAKER was born about 1950 in Elmira, Chemung, New York, USA. She married (1) WALTER JONES. He was born about 1950 in Elmira, Chemung, New York, USA. She married (2) HAAS. He was born in 1950 in (Likely), Corning, Steuben, New York, USA.

ii. JOHN SHOEMAKER was born about 1952 in Elmira, Chemung, New York, USA. He married DIANNE STRATTON SMITH. She was born about 1950 in Elmira, Chemung, New York, USA.

iii. BARBARA SHOEMAKER was born in 1958 in Elmira, Chemung, New York, USA. She married BRETT CLAUSSEN. He was born about 1958 in Elmira, Chemung, New York, USA.

58. **JOAN LOIS[5] SHOEMAKER** (Audrey Ruth[4] Fleming, Clarence Uriel Simcoe Bronte[3] Fleming, Samuel[2] Fleming, Daniel[1] Fleming) was born on 24 Oct 1926 in Elmira, Chemung, New York, USA. She died on 15 May 2005 in Rochester, Monroe, New York, USA. She married John Botsford Wilder, son of Hugo Traugott Wilder and Barbara Mary Botsford, on 18 Jun 1949 in Hammondsport, Steuben, New York, USA. He was born about 1927 in New Jersey, USA.

John Botsford Wilder and Joan Lois Shoemaker had the following children:

i.   ELIZABETH ANNE[6] WILDER was born in May 1953 in (Likely), Oneonta, Otsego, New York, USA.

80. ii. SUSAN PATRICIA WILDER was born about 1954 in (Likely), Rochester, Monroe, New York, USA. She married John M Doelp on 14 Aug 1982 in Hammondsport, Steuben, New York, USA. He was born about 1950 in (Likely), New York, USA.

81. iii. JEFFREY L WILDER was born on 28 Jun 1957 in (Likely), Rochester, Monroe, New York, USA. He married Eva Marie Lyon on 26 Jul 1986 in Beach Haven, Ocean, New Jersey, USA. She was born in Oct 1945 in (Likely), Rochester, Monroe, New York, USA.

59. **AUDREY PATRICIA[5] SHOEMAKER** (Audrey Ruth[4] Fleming, Clarence Uriel Simcoe Bronte[3] Fleming, Samuel[2] Fleming, Daniel[1] Fleming) was born on 11 May 1928 in Elmira, Chemung, New York, USA. She died on 08 Mar 2001 in Mount Vernon, Skagit, Washington, USA. She married (1) **DAVID BAIRD STORY**, son of George Hall Story Jr and Milla Marcella Baird, on 18 Aug 1951 in Bath, Steuben, New York, USA. He was born on 31 Dec 1926 in Rochester, Monroe, New York, USA. He died on 11 Oct 2001 in Longview, Cowlitz, Washington, USA (Hospice Care Centre). She married (2) **HOLLIS CHESTER WARNER** on 04 Nov 1978 in King, Washington, USA. He was born on 13 Nov 1914 in Seattle, King, Washington, USA (Father: Chester Arthur Warner (1881-1960) / Mother: Maud Arlin Northey (1885-1960)). He died on 15 Dec 1980 in Belleview, King City, Washington, Oregon, USA.

David Baird Story and Audrey Patricia Shoemaker had the following children:

i.   STEPHEN BAIRD[6] STORY was born on 21 Jun 1953 in (Likely), Steuben, Oneida, New York, USA. He married Corinne Lucille Carlisle, daughter of Leland Dale Carlisle and Eleanor Fern Godfrey, on 13 Aug 1977 in King, Washington, USA. She was born on 23 Sep 1956 in (Likely), Washington, USA.

ii. MICHAEL STORY was born about 17 Sep 1955 in (Likely), Steuben, Oneida, New York, USA.

iii. NANCY STORY was born on 14 Mar 1956 in (Likely), Steuben, Oneida, New York, USA. She married David Whitmore on 15 Sep 1979 in Multnomah, Oregon, USA. He was born about 1956 in (Likely), Longview, Cowlitz, Washington, USA.

60. **WILLIAM KEITH[5] FORBES** (Vera Aloha[4] Holmes, Sarah Felicia Louisa Pell[3] Fleming, Samuel[2] Fleming, Daniel[1] Fleming) was born on 28 May 1917 in Toronto, Ontario, Canada. He died on 16 Jul 2001 in Mississauga, Niagara, Ontario, Canada. He married Eleanor Margaret Meyer, daughter of Albert John Meyer and Margaret Mary Jacobs, on 26 Sep 1946 in Toronto, Ontario, Canada. She was born on 08 Apr 1918 in Seattle, King, Washington, USA. She died on 01 Nov 2002 in Toronto, Ontario, Canada (St

Joseph's Health Centre).

William Keith Forbes and Eleanor Margaret Meyer had the following children:

82.   i.   KEITHA JANE⁶ FORBES was born on 26 Feb 1954 in Toronto, Ontario, Canada (Keitha Jane Forbes was born on February 26, 1954 at St. Joseph's Hospital to Eleanor Margaret Meyer, age 35 and William Keith Forbes, age 36. At that time their home address was 123 Lakeshore Blvd. Toronto, Ontario.). She married Wayne Buckingham, son of Roy Buckingham and Margaret Allan Collins, on 21 Apr 1977 in Toronto, Ontario, Canada. He was born on 22 Feb 1953 in Toronto, Ontario, Canada.

83.   ii.   SUZANNE FELICIA FORBES was born on 17 Jul 1956 in Toronto, Ontario, Canada. She married Ota Josef Pokorny on 08 Apr 1978. He was born on 23 Feb 1952 in Chechoslovakia.

84.   iii.   GREGORY ARTHUR FORBES was born on 22 Sep 1959 in Toronto, Ontario, Canada. He married ALICE ROGACKI. She was born in 1954 in (Likely), Toronto, Ontario, Canada.

61.   **HELEN ROSEMARY HOLMES** (John Gumser⁴, Sarah Felicia Louisa Pell³ Fleming, Samuel² Fleming, Daniel¹ Fleming) was born on 13 Dec 1916 in Ontario, Canada. She died on 21 Nov 2013 in Toronto, Ontario, Canada (Cedarbrook Lodge). She married **ARTHUR EDWARD CORBEAU**. He was born on 18 Nov 1905 in Ontario, Canada (Father: Charles Edmund Corbeau (1881-1938) / Mother: Jane Doyle (1874-1948)). He died in 1981 in Toronto, Ontario, Canada.

Arthur Edward Corbeau and Helen Rosemary Holmes had the following child:

85.   i.   ANTHONY CORBEAU was born about 1930 in (Likely), Toronto, Ontario, Canada. He married DONNA MARGARET (). She was born about 1930 in (Likely), Toronto, Ontario, Canada.

62.   **RICHARD JAMES⁵ MARTIN** (Joseph Lacy⁴, Jasper F³, Mary Ann² Fleming, Daniel¹ Fleming) was born on 04 May 1939 in Sioux City, Woodbury, Iowa, USA. He died on 31 Oct 2011 in Berea, Madison, Kentucky, USA. He married **JUDITH FAYE STEWART**. She was born about 1945 in (Likely), Kentucky, USA. She died on 01 Jan 2017 in Berea, Madison, Kentucky, USA (She started a nonprofit to empower rural Appalachian communities.).

Richard James Martin and Judith Faye Stewart had the following children:

86.   i.   KIMMERY DAWN⁶ MARTIN was born on 13 Apr 1972 in Lexington, Fayette, Kentucky, USA. She married James Edward Fleischli on 07 Sep 2002 in Mecklenburg, North Carolina, USA. He was born on 12 Jun 1968 in (Likely), Louisville, Jefferson, Kentucky, USA.

        ii.   UNKNOWN MARTIN was born about 1990 in (Likely), Kentucky, USA.

63.   **JOSEPH VARDEMAN⁵ MARTIN** (Joseph Lacy⁴, Jasper F³, Mary Ann² Fleming, Daniel¹ Fleming) was born on 12 Nov 1911 in Vermillion, Clay, South Dakota, USA. He died on 02 Apr 1997 in Lexington, Fayette, Kentucky, USA. He married (1) **JANE SOPHIE GROVER**, daughter of Clarence Wesley Grover and Sophia Pauline Hawlish, on 15 Feb 1941 in Northwood, Worth, Iowa, USA. She was born on 31 Jan 1918 in Minneapolis, Hennepin, Minnesota, USA. She died on 30 May 1979 in Lexington, Fayette, Kentucky, USA. He married (2) **SHIRLEY ANN WAMSLEY** on 06 Nov 1937 in Minneapolis, Hennepin, Minnesota, USA. She was born about 1916. She died on 05 Feb 1996 in Waukesha, Wisconsin, USA. He married (3) **LILLIAN FRANCES HOLLAND**, daughter of William R Holland Jr and Lucretia U Lively, on 18 May 1985 in Fayette, Kentucky, USA. She was born on 07 Oct 1917 in Adams, Decatur, Indiana, USA (Father: William Russell "Willie" Holland (1895-1958) / Mother: Lucretia Uletha Lively (1897-1990)). She died on 16 Aug 2003.

Joseph Vardeman Martin and Jane Sophie Grover had the following children:

        i.   LYNNE JANE⁶ MARTIN was born on 02 Nov 1941 in Hennepin, Minnesota, USA. She married John Robert Mathias, son of Howard Miller and Genevieve Mathias, on 01 Jun 1963 in Clay, South Dakota, USA. He was born about 1942 in (Likely),

Pennington, South Dakota, USA.

ii. ROXANNE MARTIN was born on 16 Aug 1948 in Hennepin, Minnesota, USA. She married Chris Morrison Crowe on 02 Dec 1989 in Lexington, Fayette, Kentucky, USA. He was born in 1953 in (Likely), Lexington, Fayette, Kentucky, USA.

iii. JOHN GROVER MARTIN was born on 11 Aug 1951 in Hennepin, Minnesota, USA. He married Elizabeth Mussetter on 24 May 1975 in Huntsville, Butler, Kentucky, USA. She was born about 1951 in (Likely), Huntsville, Butler, Kentucky, USA.

64. ELIZABETH BROCK⁵ GILLESPIE (Elizabeth Perry⁴ Martin, Edward Daniel³ Martin, Mary Ann² Fleming, Daniel¹ Fleming) was born in 1906 in Toronto, Ontario, Canada. She married (1) CLIFFORD SIFTON in 1962. He was born in 1893. He died in 1976 in Toronto, Ontario, Canada. She married (2) FRANCIS HERBERT CRISPO, son of Frank William Sidney Crispo and Mary Louise Gertrude Tiffany, on 10 Oct 1931 in Toronto, Ontario, Canada. He was born on 02 Oct 1899 in Toronto, Ontario, Canada. He died in 1960.

Francis Herbert Crispo and Elizabeth Brock Gillespie had the following child:

87. i. JOHN HERBERT⁶ CRISPO was born on 05 May 1933 in Toronto, Ontario, Canada. He died on 27 Apr 2009 in Toronto, Ontario, Canada (Princess Margaret Hospital after an 18-year-battle with cancer.). He married (1) BARBARA () about 2000 in Creemore, Simcoe, Ontario, Canada. She was born about 1933 in (Likely), Toronto, Ontario, Canada. He married (2) MELBA TANNER. She was born about 1933 in (Likely), Toronto, Ontario, Canada.

65. CAMPBELL MARTIN⁵ MACLACHLAN (Jean Agnes⁴ Martin, Edward Daniel³ Martin, Mary Ann² Fleming, Daniel¹ Fleming) was born on 24 Jan 1917 in Winnipeg, Manitoba, Canada. He died on 06 Mar 1997 in Beaverton, Durham, Ontario, Canada. He married Mary Patricia Louise Oxley, daughter of Duncan M Oxley and Patricia Robt Boyd, about 1946 in (Likely), Toronto, Ontario, Canada. She was born on 21 Jan 1915 in Toronto, Ontario, Canada. She died on 14 Jan 1983 in Ontario, Canada.

Campbell Martin MacLachlan and Mary Patricia Louise Oxley had the following children:

i. EDWARD CAMPBELL⁶ MACLACHLAN was born on 19 Mar 1947 in Toronto, Ontario, Canada. He died on 20 Mar 1947 in Toronto, Ontario, Canada.

ii. J LOUISE MACLACHLAN was born about 1948 in (Likely), Toronto, Ontario, Canada.

66. DAVID ALEXANDER⁵ MACLACHLAN (Jean Agnes⁴ Martin, Edward Daniel³ Martin, Mary Ann² Fleming, Daniel¹ Fleming) was born on 28 Oct 1925 in Winnipeg, Manitoba, Canada. He died in 2000 in Oakville, Halton, Ontario, Canada. He married Margaret Jean Gunn on 09 Jan 1953 in Vancouver, British Columbia, Canada. She was born on 09 May 1928 in Vancouver, British Columbia, Canada.

David Alexander MacLachlan and Margaret Jean Gunn had the following children:

i. EDWARD CAMPBELL⁶ MACLACHLAN was born on 13 Oct 1954 in Vancouver, British Columbia, Canada. He died on 08 Feb 2009 in Sarnia, Lambton, Ontario, Canada.

ii. MARY MACLACHLAN was born on 20 Aug 1958 in (Likely), Sarnia, Lambton, Ontario, Canada. She died on 16 Jun 2020 in Vancouver, British Columbia, Canada. She met KENT (). He was born about 1958 in (Likely), Oakville, Halton, Ontario, Canada.

iii. KATHERINE MACLACHLAN was born about 1960 in (Likely), Sarnia, Lambton, Ontario, Canada. She married MICHAEL (). He was born about 1960 in (Likely), Sarnia, Lambton, Ontario, Canada.

iv. DIANE MACLACHLAN was born about 1960 in (Likely), Sarnia, Lambton, Ontario, Canada.

v. CAROLYN MACLACHLAN was born about 1960 in (Likely), Sarnia, Lambton, Ontario, Canada. She married PETER (). He was born about 1960 in (Likely), Sarnia, Lambton, Ontario, Canada.

vi. STEVEN MACLACHLAN was born about 1960 in (Likely), Sarnia, Lambton, Ontario, Canada.

vii. GRAHAM DAVID MACLACHLAN was born on 12 Feb 1970 in Sarnia, Lambton, Ontario,

Canada. He died about 2007 in Toronto, Ontario, Canada.

67. **KENNETH ROGER**[5] **NAIRN** (Mary Fleming[4] Martin, Edward Daniel[3] Martin, Mary Ann[2] Fleming, Daniel[1] Fleming) was born about 1923 in Rockcliffe Park, Vancouver, British Columbia, Canada. He died on 10 Jun 2006 in Vancouver, British Columbia, Canada. He married Sarah Elizabeth Gwendoline Wallace, daughter of James F A Wallace, on 08 Dec 1945 in Rockcliffe Park, Ottawa, Ontario, Canada. She was born about 1923 in (Likely), Vancouver, British Columbia, Canada. She died after 2006.

Kenneth Roger Nairn and Sarah Elizabeth Gwendoline Wallace had the following children:

    i.   JOHN ROGER[6] NAIRN was born on 15 Mar 1948 in Vancouver, British Columbia, Canada. He married Josephine Mary Sanford, daughter of A S Sanford and Sewell, on 09 Apr 1977 in Drummond Dr, Vancouver, British Columbia, Canada. She was born about 1950 in (Likely), Vancouver, British Columbia, Canada.

    ii.   DAVID KENNETH NAIRN was born about 1950 in (Likely), Vancouver, British Columbia, Canada. He married Ila Marlaine Lundy, daughter of Beldon Johnson Lundy and Ila Demaris Dorland, on 15 Jul 1977 in Unity Church, Vancouver, British Columbia, Canada. She was born about 1950 in (Likely), Vancouver, British Columbia, Canada.

    iii.   MARY NAIRN was born about 1955 in (Likely), Vancouver, British Columbia, Canada. She married GORDON (). He was born about 1950 in (Likely), Vancouver, British Columbia, Canada.

    iv.   MARK JAMES NAIRN was born about 1958 in (Likely), Vancouver, British Columbia, Canada. He married Sally Povey Walters, daughter of Herbert Thomas Harvey Walters and Audrey Jean Povey, in Aug 1983 in Vancouver, British Columbia, Canada. She was born about 1958 in (Likely), Vancouver, British Columbia, Canada.

68. **JOYCE ANN**[5] **OSBORNE** (Anna Joyce[4] White, Anna Davenport[3] Keeler, Lucy A[2] Fleming, Daniel[1] Fleming) was born on 26 Jul 1933 in Wichita, Sedgwick, Kansas, USA. She died about Sep 2017 in Gila, Arizona, USA. She married Melvin Monroe Montgomery, son of James Monroe Montgomery and Ula May Hobbs, on 31 Jan 1953 in Peridot, Gila, Arizona, USA (met her husband Melvin Montgomery at the Justa Café in Globe.). He was born on 03 Aug 1931 in Oklahoma, USA. He died on 06 Sep 2015 in Mesa, Maricopa, Arizona, USA.

Melvin Monroe Montgomery and Joyce Ann Osborne had the following children:

88.   i.   CHERYL ANNE[6] "MEZDULENE BLISS" MONTGOMERY was born in 1954 in Dayton, Montgomery, Ohio, USA. She married (1) MARTIN MCKINLEY WEDDLE. He was born on 06 Feb 1953 in Arizona, USA. She married (2) DONALD THEODORE REED JR on 23 Aug 1995 in Washoe, Nevada, USA. He was born on 04 Jan 1959 in (Likely), Oregon, USA. She married (3) STEVEN RUSSELL CUMMINS. He was born on 21 Apr 1949 in Oregon, USA.

89.   ii.   JULIA LYNN MONTGOMERY was born on 31 Dec 1957 in San Diego, California, USA. She married WILLIAM BATEMAN. He was born about 1957 in (Likely), Colorado, USA.

90.   iii.   DIANA GAIL MONTGOMERY was born on 07 Nov 1959 in San Diego, California, USA.

    iv.   SANDRA LEE MONTGOMERY was born on 21 May 1963 in San Diego, California, USA.

69. **MARILEW**[5] **WHITE** (Lewis Burton[4], Anna Davenport[3] Keeler, Lucy A[2] Fleming, Daniel[1] Fleming) was born on 06 Jan 1932 in Nebraska, USA. She died on 17 May 2011 in Yadkinville, Yadkin, North Carolina, USA. She married (1) **BERNARD LEROY VAUGHN**, son of Timothy Bernard Vaughn and Lydia Belle Viles, about 1958 (2nd marriage). He was born on 01 Aug 1928 in Topeka, Shawnee, Kansas, USA. He died on 18 Nov 2012 in Topeka, Shawnee, Kansas, USA. She married (2) **ROY J SCHELLER** on 19 Dec 1949 in Topeka, Shawnee, Kansas, USA (1st marriage). He was born on 16 Aug 1926 in Racine, Racine, Wisconsin, USA. She married (3) **EUGENE H BLOCKER** on 23 Nov 1967 (3rd marriage). He was born on 15 Mar 1936 in Georgia, USA. She married (4) **WILLIAM HEMRICK**. He was born about 1932.

Bernard Leroy Vaughn and Marilew White had the following child:

    i.   BERNARD LEROY[6] BLOCKER VAUGHN was born on 11 Oct 1959 in Topeka, Shawnee, Kansas, USA. He died in Jul 1993 in Topeka, Shawnee, Kansas, USA.

70.   **JAMES LEWIS[5] WHITE** (Lewis Burton[4], Anna Davenport[3] Keeler, Lucy A[2] Fleming, Daniel[1] Fleming) was born about 1936 in Topeka, Shawnee, Kansas, USA. He died on 23 Jan 2018 in Junction City, Geary, Kansas, USA. He married Ruby Fay Millard, daughter of Reuben West Millard and Belva A Roth, on 02 Jul 1959 (Introduced together by sister Mary Lou Hemrick.). She was born on 14 Mar 1931 in Geneseo, Rice, Kansas, USA (Father: Reuben W. Millard (1891-) / Mother: Belva A. Roth (1903-)). She died on 13 Aug 2018 in Bentley, Sedgwick, Kansas, USA.

James Lewis White and Ruby Fay Millard had the following children:

    i.   MICHAEL L[6] WHITE was born in May 1961 in (Likely) Kansas, USA. He married ELIZABETH (). She was born about 1963 in (Likely), Kansas, USA.

    ii.   JOHN P WHITE was born on 06 Sep 1964 in Topeka, Shawnee, Kansas, USA. He married CATHERINE (). She was born about 1963 in Topeka, Shawnee, Kansas, USA.

71.   **THOMAS BURT WHITE** (Lewis Burton[4], Anna Davenport[3] Keeler, Lucy A[2] Fleming, Daniel[1] Fleming) was born on 06 Feb 1945 in Topeka, Shawnee, Kansas, USA. He died on 19 Aug 2013 in Tecumseh, Shawnee, Kansas, USA. He married (1) **JANICE ALICE JESSOP**. She was born on 07 Jul 1947 in Topeka, Shawnee, Kansas, USA (Father: Wayne Winfred Jessop (1907-1967) / Mother: Beryl Beatrice Disney (1911-2004)). She died on 06 Feb 2013 in Topeka, Shawnee, Kansas, USA. He married (2) **SANDRA SUSAN BIGHAM** about 1968. She was born on 30 Aug 1941 in Brownsville, Cameron, Texas, USA (Father: Howard Raymond Bigham (1906-1977) / Mother: Iona Mae "Tony" Brown (1912-1993)). She died on 16 Mar 2010 in Marysville, Snohomish, Washington, USA. He married (3) **LILA MAY BRITTAIN DEJARNETTE** on 21 Aug 1976 in Elko, Elko, Nevada, USA. She was born about 1945 in (Likely), Kansas, USA.

Thomas Burt White had the following children:

    i.   JENNIFER NEELEY WHITE TINSLEY was born on 20 Aug 1973 in (Likely), Kansas, USA. She married (1) RANDY RIDGWAY. He was born on 25 Jan 1976 in (Likely), Kansas, USA. She married (2) NATHANIEL TINSLEY. He was born about 1975.

    ii.   DANIEL WHITE was born on 25 Oct 1975. He married JUDITH VANDYNE. She was born about 1975.

    iii.   AMY JO WHITE was born on 21 Mar 1979 in Kansas, USA. She married KARL SCHROEDER. He was born on 11 Sep 1975.

Thomas Burt White and Janice Alice Jessop had the following child:

    iv.   STACEY L CARR was born on 12 Jul 1964 in (Likely), Kansas, USA. She married TODD HOTTMAN. He was born about 1965 in (Likely), Kansas, USA.

Thomas Burt White and Sandra Susan Bigham had the following child:

91.   v.   MARCI A WHITE was born on 20 Nov 1969 in (Likely), Kansas, USA. She married (1) GREGORY W HURST on 26 Feb 2000 in Clark, Nevada, USA. He was born in Aug 1970 in (Likely), California, USA. She married (2) DANIEL L FIORILLO KEIPER on 18 Aug 2015 in Snohomish, Washington, USA. He was born about 1970 in Chehalis, Lewis, Washington, USA.

Generation 6

72.   **JONATHAN MARSH[6] HORNBLOWER** (Marjorie[5] Lloyd-Smith, Marjorie[4] Fleming, Arthur Samuel Henry[3] Fleming, Samuel[2] Fleming, Daniel[1] Fleming) was born about 1943 in (Likely), Washington, District of Columbia, USA. He married Alexandra Cheston Tower, daughter of Whitney Tower and Frances Cheston, on 29 May 1971 in Bedford, Westchester, New York, USA. She was born on 21 Apr 1949 in Ohio, USA.

Jonathan Marsh Hornblower and Alexandra Cheston Tower had the following child:

i.   JOSIAH CHESTON[7] HORNBLOWER was born on 13 Oct 1975 in Travis, Texas, USA.

73.   **GEOFFREY BLAIR[6] KERRIGAN** (Harold Fleming[5], Frances Maud[4] Fleming, Oscar Ernest[3] Fleming LLD, Samuel[2] Fleming, Daniel[1] Fleming) was born about 1946 in (Likely), Toronto, Ontario, Canada. He died on 12 Oct 2020 in Georgian Bay, Ontario, Canada (Cause of Death: Cancer). He married Heather () in 1968.

Geoffrey Blair Kerrigan and Heather () had the following children:

i.   BROOKE[7] KERRIGAN was born about 1965. She married JOHN (). He was born about 1965.

ii.   MAX KERRIGAN was born about 1965. He married PAIGE (). She was born about 1965.

74.   **CAROLYN[6] KERRIGAN MD** (Peter Frederick[5], Frances Maud[4] Fleming, Oscar Ernest[3] Fleming LLD, Samuel[2] Fleming, Daniel[1] Fleming) was born about 1950 in (Likely), Westmount, Montréal (Urban Agglomeration), Quebec, Canada. She married (1) **LINTON**. He was born about 1950 in (Likely), Montréal, Montréal (Urban Agglomeration), Quebec, Canada. She married (2) **WARREN YOUNG SOPER III**, son of Warren Young Soper II and P Claude Duval, on 18 Aug 1973 in Knowlton, Brome-Missisquoi, Quebec, Canada (in home of bride's parents). He was born about 1950 in (Likely), Montréal, Montréal (Urban Agglomeration), Quebec, Canada.

Linton and Carolyn Kerrigan MD had the following child:

i.   ELBERT NEWSON[7] LINTON was born about 1980 in (Likely), Ottawa, Ontario, Canada.

Warren Young Soper III and Carolyn Kerrigan MD had the following child:

i.   ELBERT NEWSON[7] LINTON was born about 1980 in (Likely), Ottawa, Ontario, Canada.

75.   **VANESSA[6] BENITZ** (Jocelyn Ann[5] Kerrigan, Frances Maud[4] Fleming, Oscar Ernest[3] Fleming LLD, Samuel[2] Fleming, Daniel[1] Fleming) was born about 1950. She married **GUY LAFRAMBOISE**. He was born about 1950.

Guy Laframboise and Vanessa Benitz had the following child:

i.   LISE ANNE[7] LAFRAMBOISE was born about 2000.

76.   **ANN BLYTHE[6] WOODD-CAHUSAC** (Jean Elizabeth[5] Fleming, Kenneth Eldon[4] Fleming, Oscar Ernest[3] Fleming LLD, Samuel[2] Fleming, Daniel[1] Fleming) was born about 1954. She married Matthew J Neary Jr, son of Matthew J Neary and Cynthia Audrey Evelyn, on 28 Oct 1995 in Greenwich, Fairfield, Connecticut, USA. He was born on 10 Apr 1954 in New York, New York, USA.

Matthew J Neary Jr and Ann Blythe Woodd-Cahusac had the following children:

i.   PAIGE[7] NEARY was born in Nov 1996 in (Likely), Greenwich, Fairfield, Connecticut, USA.

ii.   JAMES MACKENZIE NEARY was born in Nov 1996 in Greenwich, Fairfield, Connecticut, USA.

77.   **LEE[6] WOODD-CAHUSAC** (Jean Elizabeth[5] Fleming, Kenneth Eldon[4] Fleming, Oscar Ernest[3] Fleming LLD, Samuel[2] Fleming, Daniel[1] Fleming) was born about 1955 in Greenwich, Fairfield, Connecticut, USA (Per facebook). She married **COWANS**. He was born about 1955.

Cowans and Lee Woodd-Cahusac had the following children:

i.   ANN[7] COWANS was born about 1980 in (Likely), Toronto, Ontario, Canada.

ii.   STEWART COWANS was born about 1980 in (Likely), Toronto, Ontario, Canada.

78.   **CAROLYN GORDON[6] CLEATHER** (Edward Gordon[5], Caroline Beatrice[4] Fleming, Oscar Ernest[3] Fleming LLD, Samuel[2] Fleming, Daniel[1] Fleming) was born in Feb 1965 in Montréal, Montréal (Urban Agglomeration), Quebec, Canada. She married **RICHARD KIEL BROOK**. He was born in Aug 1959 in Beaconsfield, Montréal (Urban Agglomeration), Quebec, Canada.

Richard Kiel Brook and Carolyn Gordon Cleather had the following children:

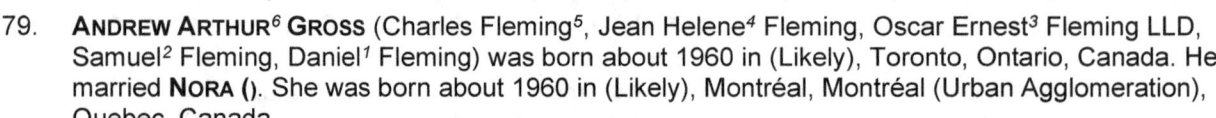

    i.   CHRISTOPHER[7] BROOK was born about 1992 in (Likely), Montréal, Montréal (Urban Agglomeration), Quebec, Canada.

    ii.   KYRA BROOK was born about 1995 in (Likely), Montréal, Montréal (Urban Agglomeration), Quebec, Canada.

    iii.   AVERY BROOK was born on 10 Apr 1999 in (Likely), Montréal, Montréal (Urban Agglomeration), Quebec, Canada. She married Abby Melton on 02 Apr 2015. She was born about 1990 in Darien, Fairfield, Connecticut, USA.

79.   **ANDREW ARTHUR[6] GROSS** (Charles Fleming[5], Jean Helene[4] Fleming, Oscar Ernest[3] Fleming LLD, Samuel[2] Fleming, Daniel[1] Fleming) was born about 1960 in (Likely), Toronto, Ontario, Canada. He married **NORA ()**. She was born about 1960 in (Likely), Montréal, Montréal (Urban Agglomeration), Quebec, Canada.

Andrew Arthur Gross and Nora () had the following children:

    i.   MAGDELENA[7] GROSS was born about 1985 in (Likely), Montréal, Montréal (Urban Agglomeration), Quebec, Canada.

    ii.   GEOFFREY GROSS was born about 1985 in (Likely), Montréal, Montréal (Urban Agglomeration), Quebec, Canada. He married SARAH ROSALIE (). She was born about 1985 in (Likely), Montréal, Montréal (Urban Agglomeration), Quebec, Canada.

    iii.   SARAH GROSS was born about 1985 in (Likely), Montréal, Montréal (Urban Agglomeration), Quebec, Canada. She married CHARLES (). He was born about 1985.

80.   **SUSAN PATRICIA[6] WILDER** (Joan Lois[5] Shoemaker, Audrey Ruth[4] Fleming, Clarence Uriel Simcoe Bronte[3] Fleming, Samuel[2] Fleming, Daniel[1] Fleming) was born about 1954 in (Likely), Rochester, Monroe, New York, USA. She married John M Doelp on 14 Aug 1982 in Hammondsport, Steuben, New York, USA. He was born about 1950 in (Likely), New York, USA.

John M Doelp and Susan Patricia Wilder had the following children:

    i.   ARTHUR[7] DOELP was born about 1996 in Darien, Fairfield, Connecticut, USA.

    ii.   JOHN DOELP was born about 1997 in (Likely), Steuben, Oneida, New York, USA.

81.   **JEFFREY L[6] WILDER** (Joan Lois[5] Shoemaker, Audrey Ruth[4] Fleming, Clarence Uriel Simcoe Bronte[3] Fleming, Samuel[2] Fleming, Daniel[1] Fleming) was born on 28 Jun 1957 in (Likely), Rochester, Monroe, New York, USA. He married Eva Marie Lyon on 26 Jul 1986 in Beach Haven, Ocean, New Jersey, USA. She was born in Oct 1945 in (Likely), Rochester, Monroe, New York, USA.

Jeffrey L Wilder and Eva Marie Lyon had the following children:

    i.   AMANDA[7] WILDER was born about 1985 in (Likely), Steuben, Oneida, New York, USA.

    ii.   JACOB WILDER was born about 1985 in (Likely), Steuben, Oneida, New York, USA.

82.   **KEITHA JANE[6] FORBES** (William Keith[5], Vera Aloha[4] Holmes, Sarah Felicia Louisa Pell[3] Fleming, Samuel[2] Fleming, Daniel[1] Fleming) was born on 26 Feb 1954 in Toronto, Ontario, Canada (Keitha Jane Forbes was born on February 26, 1954 at St. Joseph's Hospital to Eleanor Margaret Meyer, age 35 and William Keith Forbes, age 36. At that time their home address was 123 Lakeshore Blvd. Toronto, Ontario.). She married Wayne Buckingham, son of Roy Buckingham and Margaret Allan Collins, on 21 Apr 1977 in Toronto, Ontario, Canada. He was born on 22 Feb 1953 in Toronto, Ontario, Canada.

Wayne Buckingham and Keitha Jane Forbes had the following children:

92.   i.   CHRISTOPHER WAYNE[7] BUCKINGHAM was born on 08 May 1981 in Oakville, Halton, Ontario, Canada (Our first child.). He married Deborah Espinola, daughter of Candido Leal Espinola and Luisa Maria Travassos, on 03 Dec

2005. She was born on 06 Feb 1968 in Ontario, Canada.

ii. DREW ROBERT BUCKINGHAM was born on 10 Jul 1986 in Etobicoke, Toronto, Ontario, Canada (Our second child.). He married Cheyanne Colleen Ritz, daughter of Ritz and Ritz, on 15 Aug 2015 in Durham, Durham, North Carolina, USA. She was born on 28 Sep 1981 in Indiana, USA.

83. SUZANNE FELICIA[6] FORBES (William Keith[5], Vera Aloha[4] Holmes, Sarah Felicia Louisa Pell[3] Fleming, Samuel[2] Fleming, Daniel[1] Fleming) was born on 17 Jul 1956 in Toronto, Ontario, Canada. She married Ota Josef Pokorny on 08 Apr 1978. He was born on 23 Feb 1952 in Chechoslovakia.

Ota Josef Pokorny and Suzanne Felicia Forbes had the following children:

i. ORIANA[7] POKORNY was born on 21 Sep 1982 in North Bay, Nipissing, Ontario, Canada.

ii. DENISE VALENTINE POKORNY was born on 14 Feb 1984 in North Bay, Nipissing, Ontario, Canada.

93. iii. SASHA JOSEF POKORNY was born on 24 Oct 1986 in North Bay, Nipissing, Ontario, Canada. He met (1) AMANDA SEYTS. He was born about 1986. He married (2) ADELE BIRD. He was born on 08 Jan 1995.

94. iv. SAMARA POKORNY was born on 24 Oct 1986 in North Bay, Nipissing, Ontario, Canada. She married Marcel Penton on 20 Jul 2010. He was born on 30 Aug 1979 in Fogo Island, Newfoundland and Labrador, Canada.

84. GREGORY ARTHUR[6] FORBES (William Keith[5], Vera Aloha[4] Holmes, Sarah Felicia Louisa Pell[3] Fleming, Samuel[2] Fleming, Daniel[1] Fleming) was born on 22 Sep 1959 in Toronto, Ontario, Canada. He married ALICE ROGACKI. She was born in 1954 in (Likely), Toronto, Ontario, Canada.

Gregory Arthur Forbes and Alice Rogacki had the following children:

95. i. ANDREW[7] FORBES was born on 27 Mar 1987 in (Likely), Toronto, Ontario, Canada.

ii. ERIN FORBES was born in Apr 1992 in (Likely), Toronto, Ontario, Canada.

85. ANTHONY CORBEAU (Helen Rosemary Holmes, John Gumser[4] Holmes, Sarah Felicia Louisa Pell[3] Fleming, Samuel[2] Fleming, Daniel[1] Fleming) was born about 1930 in (Likely), Toronto, Ontario, Canada. He married DONNA MARGARET (). She was born about 1930 in (Likely), Toronto, Ontario, Canada.

Anthony Corbeau and Donna Margaret () had the following child:

96. i. LINDA BERNARD was born about 1955 in (Likely), Toronto, Ontario, Canada. She married ROBERT BUCHAN. He was born about 1955 in (Likely), Toronto, Ontario, Canada.

86. KIMMERY DAWN[6] MARTIN (Richard James[5], Joseph Lacy[4], Jasper F[3], Mary Ann[2] Fleming, Daniel[1] Fleming) was born on 13 Apr 1972 in Lexington, Fayette, Kentucky, USA. She married James Edward Fleischli on 07 Sep 2002 in Mecklenburg, North Carolina, USA. He was born on 12 Jun 1968 in (Likely), Louisville, Jefferson, Kentucky, USA.

James Edward Fleischli and Kimmery Dawn Martin had the following children:

i. EMMY[7] FLEISCHLI was born in 2004 in Charlotte, Mecklenburg, North Carolina, USA.

ii. ALEXANDER FLEISCHLI was born in 2006 in Charlotte, Mecklenburg, North Carolina, USA.

iii. ANN FLEISCHLI was born on 14 Sep 2010 in Charlotte, Mecklenburg, North Carolina, USA.

87. **JOHN HERBERT**[6] **CRISPO** (Elizabeth Brock[5] Gillespie, Elizabeth Perry[4] Martin, Edward Daniel[3] Martin, Mary Ann[2] Fleming, Daniel[1] Fleming) was born on 05 May 1933 in Toronto, Ontario, Canada. He died on 27 Apr 2009 in Toronto, Ontario, Canada (Princess Margaret Hospital after an 18-year-battle with cancer.). He married (1) **BARBARA ()** about 2000 in Creemore, Simcoe, Ontario, Canada. She was born about 1933 in (Likely), Toronto, Ontario, Canada. He married (2) **MELBA TANNER**. She was born about 1933 in (Likely), Toronto, Ontario, Canada.

John Herbert Crispo and Barbara () had the following child:

    i.   MATHEW[7] BRODKIN was born about 1955. He married LESLEY CLEMENTS. She was born about 1955 in (Likely), Toronto, Ontario, Canada.

John Herbert Crispo and Melba Tanner had the following children:

97.   ii.   SHARON CRISPO was born about 1955 in (Likely), Toronto, Ontario, Canada. She married BRIAN LINES. He was born about 1955 in (Likely), Toronto, Ontario, Canada.

98.   iii.   CAROL ANN CRISPO was born about 1955 in (Likely), Toronto, Ontario, Canada. She died on 20 Aug 2009 in Toronto, Ontario, Canada (Cause of Death: breast cancer). She married TWIGG. He was born about 1955 in Toronto, Ontario, Canada.

88. **CHERYL ANNE**[6] **"MEZDULENE BLISS" MONTGOMERY** (Joyce Ann[5] Osborne, Anna Joyce[4] White, Anna Davenport[3] Keeler, Lucy A[2] Fleming, Daniel[1] Fleming) was born in 1954 in Dayton, Montgomery, Ohio, USA. She married (1) **MARTIN MCKINLEY WEDDLE**. He was born on 06 Feb 1953 in Arizona, USA. She married (2) **DONALD THEODORE REED JR** on 23 Aug 1995 in Washoe, Nevada, USA. He was born on 04 Jan 1959 in (Likely), Oregon, USA. She married (3) **STEVEN RUSSELL CUMMINS**. He was born on 21 Apr 1949 in Oregon, USA.

Martin McKinley Weddle and Cheryl Anne "Mezdulene Bliss" Montgomery had the following child:

99.   i.   AVENA ANNE[7] WEDDLE was born on 21 Mar 1976 in Coos Bay, Coos, Oregon, USA. She married Yashveer Singh on 24 May 2002 in Coos, Oregon, USA. He was born on 28 May 1977.

Steven Russell Cummins and Cheryl Anne "Mezdulene Bliss" Montgomery had the following child:

    i.   LOGAN SCOTT[7] CUMMINS was born on 26 Nov 1989 in Coos Bay, Coos, Oregon, USA.

89. **JULIA LYNN**[6] **MONTGOMERY** (Joyce Ann[5] Osborne, Anna Joyce[4] White, Anna Davenport[3] Keeler, Lucy A[2] Fleming, Daniel[1] Fleming) was born on 31 Dec 1957 in San Diego, California, USA. She married **WILLIAM BATEMAN**. He was born about 1957 in (Likely), Colorado, USA.

William Bateman and Julia Lynn Montgomery had the following child:

    i.   JENNA[7] BATEMAN was born about 1990 in (Likely), Arizona, USA. She married JACOB TIMOTHY BODMER. He was born in Mar 1989 in (Likely), Colorado, USA.

90. **DIANA GAIL**[6] **MONTGOMERY** (Joyce Ann[5] Osborne, Anna Joyce[4] White, Anna Davenport[3] Keeler, Lucy A[2] Fleming, Daniel[1] Fleming) was born on 07 Nov 1959 in San Diego, California, USA.

Diana Gail Montgomery had the following child:

    i.   KEIRA[7] MONTGOMERY was born about 1993 in China.

91. **MARCI A WHITE** (Thomas Burt, Lewis Burton[4], Anna Davenport[3] Keeler, Lucy A[2] Fleming, Daniel[1] Fleming) was born on 20 Nov 1969 in (Likely), Kansas, USA. She married (1) **GREGORY W HURST** on 26 Feb 2000 in Clark, Nevada, USA. He was born in Aug 1970 in (Likely), California, USA. She married (2) **DANIEL L FIORILLO KEIPER** on 18 Aug 2015 in Snohomish, Washington, USA. He was born about 1970 in Chehalis, Lewis, Washington, USA.

Gregory W Hurst and Marci A White had the following children:

    i.   JOSHUA HURST was born about 2003 in (Likely), Washington, USA.

ii. UNKNOWN HURST.

Daniel L Fiorillo Keiper and Marci A White had the following children:

i. JOSHUA HURST was born about 2003 in (Likely), Washington, USA.

ii. UNKNOWN HURST.

Generation 7

92. **CHRISTOPHER WAYNE**[7] **BUCKINGHAM** (Keitha Jane[6] Forbes, William Keith[5] Forbes, Vera Aloha[4] Holmes, Sarah Felicia Louisa Pell[3] Fleming, Samuel[2] Fleming, Daniel[1] Fleming) was born on 08 May 1981 in Oakville, Halton, Ontario, Canada (Our first child.). He married Deborah Espinola, daughter of Candido Leal Espinola and Luisa Maria Travassos, on 03 Dec 2005. She was born on 06 Feb 1968 in Ontario, Canada.

Christopher Wayne Buckingham and Deborah Espinola had the following child:

i. JACOB ESPINOLA[8] BUCKINGHAM was born on 03 Jul 2005 in Brampton, Peel, Ontario, Canada.

93. **SASHA JOSEF**[7] **POKORNY** (Suzanne Felicia[6] Forbes, William Keith[5] Forbes, Vera Aloha[4] Holmes, Sarah Felicia Louisa Pell[3] Fleming, Samuel[2] Fleming, Daniel[1] Fleming) was born on 24 Oct 1986 in North Bay, Nipissing, Ontario, Canada. He met (1) **AMANDA SEYTS**. He was born about 1986. He married (2) **ADELE BIRD**. He was born on 08 Jan 1995.

Amanda Seyts and Sasha Josef Pokorny had the following child:

i. RONAN JOSEF[8] POKORNY was born on 09 Oct 2016 in North Bay, Nipissing, Ontario, Canada.

Adele Bird and Sasha Josef Pokorny had the following child:

i. AUGUST BRANDON[8] POKORNY was born on 16 Oct 2021 in North Bay, Nipissing, Ontario, Canada.

94. **SAMARA**[7] **POKORNY** (Suzanne Felicia[6] Forbes, William Keith[5] Forbes, Vera Aloha[4] Holmes, Sarah Felicia Louisa Pell[3] Fleming, Samuel[2] Fleming, Daniel[1] Fleming) was born on 24 Oct 1986 in North Bay, Nipissing, Ontario, Canada. She married Marcel Penton on 20 Jul 2010. He was born on 30 Aug 1979 in Fogo Island, Newfoundland and Labrador, Canada.

Marcel Penton and Samara Pokorny had the following child:

i. RORY OTA[8] PENTON was born on 03 Nov 2013 in Fogo Island, Newfoundland and Labrador, Canada.

95. **ANDREW**[7] **FORBES** (Gregory Arthur[6], William Keith[5], Vera Aloha[4] Holmes, Sarah Felicia Louisa Pell[3] Fleming, Samuel[2] Fleming, Daniel[1] Fleming) was born on 27 Mar 1987 in (Likely), Toronto, Ontario, Canada.

Andrew Forbes had the following child:

i. ELEANOR[8] FORBES was born about 2010 in (Likely), Vancouver, British Columbia, Canada.

96. **LINDA BERNARD** (Anthony Corbeau, Helen Rosemary Holmes, John Gumser[4] Holmes, Sarah Felicia Louisa Pell[3] Fleming, Samuel[2] Fleming, Daniel[1] Fleming) was born about 1955 in (Likely), Toronto, Ontario, Canada. She married **ROBERT BUCHAN**. He was born about 1955 in (Likely), Toronto, Ontario, Canada.

Robert Buchan and Linda Bernard had the following child:

100. i. SLOANE BERNARD was born about 1983 in (Likely), Toronto, Ontario, Canada. She married TROY ASSELIN. He was born about 1980 in (Likely), Toronto, Ontario, Canada.

97. **SHARON**[7] **CRISPO** (John Herbert[6], Elizabeth Brock[5] Gillespie, Elizabeth Perry[4] Martin, Edward Daniel[3] Martin, Mary Ann[2] Fleming, Daniel[1] Fleming) was born about 1955 in (Likely), Toronto, Ontario, Canada. She married **BRIAN LINES**. He was born about 1955 in (Likely), Toronto, Ontario, Canada.

Brian Lines and Sharon Crispo had the following children:

    i.   NICHOLAS[8] LINES was born about 1990 in (Likely), Toronto, Ontario, Canada.

    ii.   BENJAMIN LINES was born about 1990 in (Likely), Toronto, Ontario, Canada.

98. **CAROL ANN**[7] **CRISPO** (John Herbert[6], Elizabeth Brock[5] Gillespie, Elizabeth Perry[4] Martin, Edward Daniel[3] Martin, Mary Ann[2] Fleming, Daniel[1] Fleming) was born about 1955 in (Likely), Toronto, Ontario, Canada. She died on 20 Aug 2009 in Toronto, Ontario, Canada (Cause of Death: breast cancer). She married **TWIGG**. He was born about 1955 in Toronto, Ontario, Canada.

Twigg and Carol Ann Crispo had the following child:

    i.   GEOFFREY[8] TWIGG was born about 1980 in (Likely), Toronto, Ontario, Canada.

99. **AVENA ANNE**[7] **WEDDLE** (Cheryl Anne[6] "Mezdulene Bliss" Montgomery, Joyce Ann[5] Osborne, Anna Joyce[4] White, Anna Davenport[3] Keeler, Lucy A[2] Fleming, Daniel[1] Fleming) was born on 21 Mar 1976 in Coos Bay, Coos, Oregon, USA. She married Yashveer Singh on 24 May 2002 in Coos, Oregon, USA. He was born on 28 May 1977.

Yashveer Singh and Avena Anne Weddle had the following children:

    i.   AAYUSH[8] SINGH was born on 31 Aug 2005 in Coos Bay, Coos, Oregon, USA.

    ii.   RISHABH SINGH was born on 25 Oct 2007 in Coos Bay, Coos, Oregon, USA.

    iii.   SAYJAL SINGH was born on 20 Nov 2013 in Coos Bay, Coos, Oregon, USA.

Generation 8

100. **SLOANE BERNARD** (Linda, Anthony Corbeau, Helen Rosemary Holmes, John Gumser[4] Holmes, Sarah Felicia Louisa Pell[3] Fleming, Samuel[2] Fleming, Daniel[1] Fleming) was born about 1983 in (Likely), Toronto, Ontario, Canada. She married **TROY ASSELIN**. He was born about 1980 in (Likely), Toronto, Ontario, Canada.

Troy Asselin and Sloane Bernard had the following children:

    i.   HENRY ASSELIN was born on 15 Aug 2013 in (Likely), Toronto, Ontario, Canada.

    ii.   CHARLOTTE ASSELIN was born about Oct 2015 in (Likely), Toronto, Ontario, Canada.

www.ingramcontent.com/pod-product-compliance
Lightning Source LLC
Chambersburg PA
CBHW081606280526
45788CB00011B/3574